AF577802

Dedicated to the curious minds of all ages, who strive to constantly expand their knowledge and explore the limitless possibilities of our world. May this book inspire you to continue asking questions, seeking answers, and never stop imagining the impossible

EXPLORING THE WHAT-IFS OF OUR WORLD: A JOURNEY THROUGH SCIENTIFIC POSSIBILITIES

SHIVAM GOEL

Copyright © Shivam Goel
All Rights Reserved.

This book has been self-published with all reasonable efforts taken to make the material error-free by the author. No part of this book shall be used, reproduced in any manner whatsoever without written permission from the author, except in the case of brief quotations embodied in critical articles and reviews.

The Author of this book is solely responsible and liable for its content including but not limited to the views, representations, descriptions, statements, information, opinions and references ["Content"]. The Content of this book shall not constitute or be construed or deemed to reflect the opinion or expression of the Publisher or Editor. Neither the Publisher nor Editor endorse or approve the Content of this book or guarantee the reliability, accuracy or completeness of the Content published herein and do not make any representations or warranties of any kind, express or implied, including but not limited to the implied warranties of merchantability, fitness for a particular purpose. The Publisher and Editor shall not be liable whatsoever for any errors, omissions, whether such errors or omissions result from negligence, accident, or any other cause or claims for loss or damages of any kind, including without limitation, indirect or consequential loss or damage arising out of use, inability to use, or about the reliability, accuracy or sufficiency of the information contained in this book.

Made with ♥ on the Notion Press Platform
www.notionpress.com

Contents

Foreword

Foreword:

It is with great pleasure that I write the foreword for "Exploring the What-Ifs of Our World: A Journey Through Scientific Possibilities." This captivating book takes us on a journey through the world of science, exploring the many "what-ifs" that have captivated human imagination for centuries.

The author has expertly woven together the latest scientific knowledge and theories with thought-provoking scenarios, resulting in a book that is not only educational, but also entertaining and thought-provoking. From the possibility of time travel to the possibility of terraforming other planets, this book delves into the depths of scientific imagination and possibility.

This book is a must-read for anyone with an interest in science and the limitless possibilities that exist within our world. Whether you are a seasoned science enthusiast or someone who is just beginning to explore the wonders of the universe, "Exploring the What-Ifs of Our World" offers an engaging and insightful journey through the unknown.

So, buckle up and join the author on this exciting journey through the what-ifs of our world. I guarantee that you will not be disappointed.

Preface

Preface:

Welcome to "Exploring the What-Ifs of Our World: A Journey Through Scientific Possibilities". This book is a collection of thought-provoking scenarios and what-ifs that delve into the realm of science fiction and science fact. The world of science has always captivated the minds of people, providing us with a glimpse into the unknown, the mysterious and the seemingly impossible. In this book, we explore the various scientific possibilities that have been proposed and speculate on what the world would be like if they were to come true.

This book takes the reader on a journey through various scientific possibilities, from the impact of a world without gravity, to the consequences of terraforming other planets. Each chapter is a detailed exploration of a specific scenario, providing an in-depth analysis of the scientific, technological and societal implications. With a focus on providing accurate scientific information and an engaging writing style, this book offers a unique perspective on the what-ifs of our world.

Whether you are a science enthusiast, a science fiction fan, or just curious about the possibilities of our world, this book will provide you with a wealth of knowledge and a new perspective on the scientific possibilities that exist. So come along with me on this journey of exploring the what-ifs of our world, and let's discover together the wonders that science has in store for us.

Acknowledgements

ACKNOWLEDGMENTS

Writing a book is never a one-person effort, and this book is no exception. I would like to extend my sincerest gratitude to all those who have helped me in bringing this book to life.

I would like to thank my editor, [Editor Name], for their invaluable support and guidance throughout the writing process. Their insights, expertise, and attention to detail were essential to shaping this book into its final form.

I am grateful to [Publishing House Name] for their support and belief in this project, and for their assistance in bringing it to a wider audience. I would also like to extend my appreciation to my literary agent, [Agent Name], for their tireless efforts in helping me navigate the publishing world.

I am deeply grateful to the many scientists, researchers, and experts who graciously shared their time and knowledge with me. Their insights helped me to understand complex scientific concepts and bring them to life for readers. I would like to extend a special thank you to [Scientist/Researcher/Expert Names], whose contribution to this book was invaluable.

Finally, I would like to acknowledge the love and support of my family and friends, who have been with me every step of the way. Their encouragement, understanding, and unwavering support have been a constant source of inspiration, and I am forever grateful.

Thank you all for your contributions to this book. It is my hope that it will inspire others to explore the wonders of science and the many what-ifs of our world.

Prologue

Prologue

The human mind has always been curious, constantly seeking answers to the unknown and imagining what could be. We dream of possibilities and question the limitations of our world, yearning for a greater understanding of what lies beyond. This is the essence of science - to seek truth, to unravel the mysteries of the universe, and to explore the boundless wonders that exist within it.

This book takes you on a journey through the scientific possibilities of our world, exploring the what-ifs and the could-bes of our existence. From the hypothetical scenarios of terraforming other planets to the possibility of time travel, we delve into the theories and possibilities that have captivated the minds of scientists and thinkers for generations.

Each chapter delves into a different topic, investigating the science behind it and exploring what would happen if these theories were to become reality. With a focus on exploring the potential impact on humanity, the book offers a fascinating look at the possibilities of our world.

As you journey through these pages, you'll encounter new and exciting ideas, each one a window into the potential future of our world. You'll discover the science behind each theory, and the impact it could have on our lives, our planet, and even the universe.

So come, join us on this journey through the what-ifs of our world. Let us be inspired by the endless possibilities of science, and let us embrace the thrill of exploring the unknown.

CHAPTER ONE

WHAT WOULD HAPPEN IF ALL THE INSECTS IN THE WORLD DISAPPEARED?

Insects play a crucial role in the ecosystem and are essential for the survival of numerous species of plants and animals. They are also vital for the pollination of crops, decomposition of organic matter, and maintaining the balance of the food chain. This Chapter will explore the consequences of a hypothetical scenario where all insects in the world suddenly disappear. The chapter will discuss the impacts of insect extinction on the ecosystem and the food chain, and how it will affect the survival of various species of plants and animals, as well as human beings.

Introduction:

Insects are one of the most abundant groups of animals on the planet and make up more than half of all known species. They play an important role in the ecosystem and are involved in several crucial processes such as pollination, decomposition, and maintaining the balance of the food chain. However, the population of insects has been declining in recent years due to factors such as habitat loss, use of pesticides, and climate change. In this chapter, we will explore the consequences of a hypothetical scenario where all insects in the world suddenly disappear.

Impacts on the Ecosystem and Food Chain:

The extinction of insects would have significant impacts on the ecosystem and the food chain. Many species of birds, reptiles, amphibians, and mammals rely on insects as a food source, and their disappearance would cause these species to struggle for survival. The extinction of pollinators such as bees, butterflies, and beetles would also have severe consequences for the survival of plants and crops, as they play a crucial role in the pollination process. The absence of insects would also mean that the decomposition of organic matter would slow down, leading to a buildup of dead plant and animal matter in the ecosystem.

Impacts on Other Species:

The extinction of insects would have a domino effect on the survival of various species of plants and animals. For example, the disappearance of caterpillars, which are a food source for birds, would lead to a decline in bird populations, which would then affect the survival of other species that rely on birds for food. Similarly, the extinction of pollinators would result in a decline in the population of plants, which would then impact the survival of animals that rely on those plants for food.

Impacts on Humans:

The extinction of insects would also have significant impacts on human beings. The decline of pollinators would result in reduced crop yields, which would lead to food shortages and increased food prices. The reduction in the number of insects involved in decomposition would also lead to increased waste, which would result in health and environmental problems. In addition, the loss of insects would also have economic impacts, as the production of honey, beeswax, and silk would decline.

Impacts on the Ecosystem and Food Chain:

Insects are essential to the functioning of the ecosystem and play a crucial role in the food chain. They act as pollinators for plants, helping to ensure their survival and reproduction. They also play a key role in the decomposition of organic matter, breaking down dead plant and animal matter and returning essential nutrients to the soil. The disappearance of insects would have a profound impact on the ecosystem and food chain.

Many species of birds, reptiles, amphibians, and mammals rely on insects as a food source. The sudden disappearance of insects would leave these species struggling to find alternative food sources, potentially leading to declines in their populations. Similarly, the extinction of pollinators such as bees, butterflies, and beetles would result in reduced crop yields and negatively impact the food supply for both humans and wildlife. The absence of insects involved in decomposition would also lead to a buildup of dead plant and animal matter in the ecosystem, potentially altering the balance of the food chain and leading to declines in populations of other species.

Impacts on Other Species:

The extinction of insects would have a domino effect on the survival of various species of plants and animals. For example, the disappearance of caterpillars, which are a food source for birds, would lead to a decline in bird populations. This in turn could negatively impact the survival of other species that rely on birds for food. The decline in the population of plants due to a lack of pollinators would also impact the survival of animals that rely on those plants for food. The extinction of insects would result in a ripple effect throughout the ecosystem, potentially leading to declines in the populations of many species.

Impacts on Humans:

The disappearance of insects would also have significant impacts on human beings. Reduced crop yields due to a lack of pollinators would result in food shortages and increased food prices, potentially leading to food insecurity for many people. The reduction in the number of insects involved in decomposition would also lead to increased waste, potentially resulting in health and environmental problems. The loss of insects would also have economic impacts, as the production of honey, beeswax, and silk would decline. These products are important sources of income for many people, and their disappearance would negatively impact local economies.

In addition to the impacts on food production and the economy, the loss of insects would also have cultural and aesthetic impacts. Insects play a role in many cultural traditions and are appreciated for their beauty and diversity by many people. The disappearance of insects would result in the loss of this diversity and cultural heritage.

The extinction of insects would have far-reaching consequences for the ecosystem, the food chain, and human beings. It is important to take action to protect insects and their habitats to ensure their survival and prevent the potential consequences of their extinction.

Impacts on Soil and Plant Life:

Insects play a vital role in soil health and plant growth. They aid in nutrient cycling by breaking down dead plant and animal matter, releasing essential nutrients back into the soil. They also play a key role in controlling plant pests, helping to maintain healthy and diverse plant communities. The disappearance of insects would result in a decline in soil fertility, leading to reduced plant growth and biodiversity.

The loss of pollinators such as bees, butterflies, and beetles would also have significant impacts on plant life. These insects play a crucial role in the pollination of flowers, ensuring the reproduction and survival of many plant species. The absence of pollinators would result in reduced crop yields and potentially lead to the extinction of some plant species. This in turn would impact the populations of animals that rely on those plants for food.

Impacts on Biodiversity:

Insects are one of the most diverse groups of animals on the planet, with over a million species described to date. They occupy a wide range of habitats and play key roles in the functioning of ecosystems. The extinction of insects would result in a significant loss of biodiversity, potentially leading to declines in the populations of other species. This could result in the loss of important ecosystem services, such as pollination, decomposition, and nutrient cycling.

The loss of insects would also have impacts on the functioning of ecosystems. For example, the absence of insects involved in decomposition would result in a buildup of dead plant and animal matter, altering the balance of the food chain and potentially leading to declines in the populations of other species. The loss of insects would also impact the predator-prey relationships that play a key role in maintaining ecosystem stability.

Impacts on Pest Control:

Insects play a crucial role in controlling plant pests, helping to maintain healthy and diverse plant communities. The disappearance of insects would result in a decline in biological control of pests, potentially leading to increased use of pesticides and other chemical controls. This in turn could result in negative impacts on the environment, including soil and water pollution and harm to non-target species. In addition, the overuse of chemical controls could lead to the development of pesticide-resistant pests, making it more difficult to control these species in the future.

Impacts on Climate and Weather:

Insects play an important role in the global carbon cycle. They help to regulate the balance of carbon in the atmosphere by participating in the process of carbon sequestration. Through their role in decomposition and nutrient cycling, insects help to store carbon in the soil and vegetation. The disappearance of insects would result in a decline in the amount of carbon stored in the soil and vegetation, potentially contributing to global warming and climate change.

In addition, insects play a role in the water cycle. They help to regulate the distribution and quality of water in the ecosystem, affecting the availability of water for plants and animals. The absence of insects would result in changes to the water cycle, potentially leading to droughts, floods, and other weather-related problems.

Impacts on Medicinal and Industrial Applications:

Insects have played a significant role in the development of many important medical and industrial applications. For example, insects have been used to produce antivenom for snake bites, and honeybees are a critical component of the pollination of many crops used in the production of medicines and other products. The disappearance of insects would result in the loss of these important applications and potentially hinder the development of new applications in the future.

In addition, insects play a key role in the production of bioplastics, which are environmentally friendly alternatives to traditional petroleum-based plastics. The disappearance of insects would reduce the availability of these materials and potentially result in increased use of traditional plastics, contributing to environmental problems such as plastic pollution.

Impacts on Human Health:

The disappearance of insects would also have significant impacts on human health. Many insects are important vectors of diseases, transmitting illnesses such as malaria, dengue fever, and yellow fever to humans. The absence of these insects would result in a decline in the incidence of these diseases, potentially improving public health. However, the loss of insects would also result in the loss of important sources of food and medicine, potentially contributing to malnutrition and health problems in some regions.

Impacts on Food Supply and Agriculture:

Insects play a crucial role in the food chain, serving as both predators and prey for many other species. They are also important pollinators, ensuring the reproduction and survival of many crops. The disappearance of insects would result in a decline in the availability of food for many species, potentially leading to declines in population levels and even extinction.

The loss of pollinators such as bees, butterflies, and beetles would have significant impacts on agriculture and food supply. These insects play a key role in the pollination of crops, helping to ensure the production of food for human consumption. The absence of pollinators would result in reduced crop yields and potentially lead to food shortages in some regions. This could have significant impacts on food security and the livelihoods of millions of people.

Impacts on Ecosystem Stability:

Insects play an important role in maintaining the stability of ecosystems by participating in key processes such as decomposition and nutrient cycling. They also play a role in predator-prey relationships, helping to regulate population levels and maintain balance in the food chain. The disappearance of insects would result in changes to these processes, potentially leading to declines in the populations of other species and disrupting the balance of the food chain.

In addition, the loss of insects would result in changes to the structure of ecosystems, potentially leading to declines in biodiversity and the loss of important ecosystem services. For example, the absence of insects involved in decomposition would result in a buildup of dead plant and animal matter, altering the balance of the food chain and potentially leading to declines in the populations of other species.

Impacts on Recreational Activities:

Insects play a role in many recreational activities, including fishing and bird watching. They are also important sources of food and medicine for many indigenous peoples. The disappearance of insects would result in the loss of these recreational and cultural activities, potentially impacting the livelihoods and cultures of many communities.

Impacts on Biodiversity:

Insects play a crucial role in maintaining biodiversity, serving as food and habitat for many other species. They are also involved in many ecosystem processes, such as pollination and decomposition, that support the survival of other species. The disappearance of insects would result in declines in the populations of many other species and potentially lead to declines in biodiversity.

In addition, insects are important indicators of ecosystem health, providing early warning signs of environmental changes. For example, declines in insect populations can signal changes in the quality of the environment, including declines in air and water quality, changes in land use practices, and the impacts of climate change. The disappearance of insects would result in the loss of these important indicators, making it more difficult to detect and respond to environmental changes.

Impacts on Soil Quality:

Insects play a crucial role in maintaining soil quality, participating in important processes such as nutrient cycling and decomposition. They help to break down dead plant and animal matter, releasing nutrients into the soil and supporting the growth of new plants. The disappearance of insects would result in a decline in soil quality, potentially reducing the productivity of agricultural lands and contributing to declines in food security.

In addition, insects play a role in controlling pests and diseases in agricultural systems, helping to maintain healthy and productive crops. The disappearance of insects would result in an increase in pest and disease problems, potentially leading to declines in crop yields and food security.

Impacts on Ecosystem Functioning:

Insects play a crucial role in maintaining the functioning of ecosystems, participating in key processes such as nutrient cycling, decomposition, and pollination. They are also involved in predator-prey relationships, helping to regulate population levels and maintain balance in the food chain. The disappearance of insects would result in changes to these processes, potentially leading to declines in the populations of other species and disrupting the balance of the food chain.

In addition, the loss of insects would result in changes to the structure of ecosystems, potentially leading to declines in biodiversity and the loss of important ecosystem services. For example, the absence of insects involved in decomposition would result in a buildup of dead plant and animal matter, altering the balance of the food chain and potentially leading to declines in the populations of other species.

Impacts on Carbon Cycling:

Insects play a role in the carbon cycle, helping to decompose organic matter and release carbon into the atmosphere. They also participate in the carbon sequestration process, helping to remove carbon from the atmosphere and store it in soils. The disappearance of insects would result in changes to the carbon cycle, potentially leading to changes in atmospheric carbon dioxide levels and contributing to global warming.

In addition, insects play a role in maintaining the health of forests and other ecosystems, helping to support the growth of trees and other vegetation that sequester carbon. The loss of insects would result in declines in the health and productivity of these ecosystems, potentially reducing their ability to sequester carbon and contributing to global warming.

Impacts on Water Quality and Availability:

Insects play a role in maintaining the quality and availability of water, participating in important processes such as nutrient cycling and decomposition. They also help to control pests and diseases in aquatic systems, helping to maintain healthy and productive ecosystems. The disappearance of insects would result in changes to these processes, potentially leading to declines in water quality and availability.

In addition, insects play a role in maintaining the health of wetlands and other aquatic ecosystems, helping to support the growth of vegetation that provides important ecosystem services such as water purification and flood control. The loss of insects would result in declines in the health and productivity of these ecosystems, potentially reducing their ability to provide these important services.

Impacts on Human Health:

Insects play a role in human health, serving as vectors for diseases such as malaria, dengue fever, and Lyme disease. They also play a role in maintaining the health of ecosystems, providing important ecosystem services such as pollination and decomposition that support human wellbeing. The disappearance of insects would result in changes to these processes, potentially leading to declines in human health and wellbeing.

In addition, insects are important sources of food and medicine for many people, providing essential nutrients and compounds that support human health. The loss of insects would result in declines in the availability of these important resources, potentially reducing the health and wellbeing of millions of people.

In conclusion, the disappearance of insects would have far-reaching and profound impacts on the functioning of ecosystems, biodiversity, and human wellbeing. Insects play critical roles in maintaining the balance of the food chain, supporting the growth of vegetation, and providing important ecosystem services such as pollination, decomposition, and disease control. The loss of insects would result in declines in biodiversity, soil quality, and water quality and availability, as well as changes to the carbon cycle and reductions in human health and wellbeing. These impacts highlight the importance of protecting and preserving insect populations, and the need for effective strategies to conserve and manage these essential components of the natural world.

CHAPTER TWO

How would our lives change if gravity were halved?

Introduction:

Gravity is one of the fundamental forces of nature, governing the motion of objects and playing a key role in shaping our environment and the structures of the universe. But what would happen if the strength of gravity were halved? This hypothetical scenario is the subject of much speculation and scientific inquiry, with scientists seeking to understand the impacts of such a change on our planet, our bodies, and our lives.

Body:

Impacts on the Earth's Environment:

A reduction in gravity would result in significant changes to the Earth's environment, including alterations to its climate, weather patterns, and geology. With less gravitational force to hold the atmosphere in place, it would expand and become more diffuse, leading to changes in atmospheric pressure and temperature. This could result in a more stable climate, with fewer extreme weather events and fewer hurricanes and tornadoes.

In addition, halving the strength of gravity would reduce the amount of erosion caused by water and wind, potentially leading to the formation of new landmasses and the preservation of existing ones. It would also reduce the amount of tectonic activity, potentially reducing the frequency of earthquakes and volcanic eruptions.

Impacts on the Human Body:

A reduction in gravity would have a profound impact on the human body, with significant changes to our biology, anatomy, and physiology. Our bodies are adapted to the strength of Earth's gravity, and a change in that force would result in changes to our musculoskeletal system, affecting our balance and posture. We would be less dense, taller, and have longer bones, potentially making us more susceptible to injury.

In addition, a reduction in gravity would affect the circulatory system, with less force needed to pump blood and circulate oxygen. This could result in changes to our heart and lung function, as well as our ability to process nutrients and waste.

Impacts on Technology and Society:

A reduction in gravity would also have significant impacts on technology and society, affecting the design and performance of vehicles, buildings, and other structures. The reduced gravitational force would make it easier to launch objects into space, potentially reducing the cost and energy required to launch satellites and other spacecraft. In addition, lighter vehicles would require less fuel and energy to operate, potentially reducing our dependence on fossil fuels and contributing to a more sustainable future.

However, halving the strength of gravity would also require significant changes to our infrastructure, with buildings, bridges, and other structures needing to be redesigned to withstand the reduced force. In addition, changes to the human body would require changes to the design of tools and machinery, potentially leading to new and innovative technologies.

Impacts on the Earth's Environment:

A reduction in gravity would result in significant changes to the Earth's environment, including alterations to its climate, weather patterns, and geology. With less gravitational force to hold the atmosphere in place, it would expand and become more diffuse, leading to changes in atmospheric pressure and temperature. This could result in a more stable climate, with fewer extreme weather events and fewer hurricanes and tornadoes.

In addition, halving the strength of gravity would reduce the amount of erosion caused by water and wind, potentially leading to the formation of new landmasses and the preservation of existing ones. It would also reduce the amount of tectonic activity, potentially reducing the frequency of earthquakes and volcanic eruptions.

Impacts on the Human Body:

A reduction in gravity would have a profound impact on the human body, with significant changes to our biology, anatomy, and physiology. Our bodies are adapted to the strength of Earth's gravity, and a change in that force would result in changes to our musculoskeletal system, affecting our balance and posture. We would be less dense, taller, and have longer bones, potentially making us more susceptible to injury.

In addition, a reduction in gravity would affect the circulatory system, with less force needed to pump blood and circulate oxygen. This could result in changes to our heart and lung function, as well as our ability to process nutrients and waste.

Impacts on Technology and Society:

A reduction in gravity would also have significant impacts on technology and society, affecting the design and performance of vehicles, buildings, and other structures. The reduced gravitational force would make it easier to launch objects into space, potentially reducing the cost and energy required to launch satellites and other spacecraft. In addition, lighter vehicles would require less fuel and energy to operate, potentially reducing our dependence on fossil fuels and contributing to a more sustainable future.

However, halving the strength of gravity would also require significant changes to our infrastructure, with buildings, bridges, and other structures needing to be redesigned to withstand the reduced force. This could result in new challenges for engineers and architects, requiring them to find new and innovative solutions for designing and building structures.

In addition, changes to the human body would require changes to the design of tools and machinery, potentially leading to new and innovative technologies. For example, lighter and more flexible tools and equipment could be developed to better match the altered physiology of the human body.

It's important to note that while halving the strength of gravity would have many potential benefits, it could also have unintended consequences. For example, it's possible that the altered environment could result in the extinction of certain species or the emergence of new diseases. Further research and analysis is needed to fully understand the impacts of such a change and to ensure that any potential benefits are realized while minimizing any negative consequences.

Impacts on Agriculture:

Agriculture would also be greatly affected by a reduction in gravity. With lighter soil and reduced erosion, new areas of land could become suitable for agriculture, potentially leading to increased food production and greater food security. At the same time, changes in the water cycle and weather patterns could also impact agriculture, requiring farmers to adapt to new growing conditions.

In addition, lighter plants and crops would be more susceptible to damage from wind and rain, potentially leading to reduced crop yields and increased costs for farmers. This would require farmers to adopt new strategies for protecting their crops, such as developing more durable varieties or using new methods for supporting plants.

Impacts on Energy Production:

Energy production would also be impacted by a reduction in gravity, with changes to the water cycle and weather patterns potentially affecting the production of hydroelectric and wind energy. In addition, lighter and more diffuse atmospheric conditions could make it easier to capture solar energy, potentially increasing the efficiency and performance of solar panels and other renewable energy technologies.

However, a reduction in gravity could also make it more difficult to extract fossil fuels and minerals, as less force would be available to pump oil and gas from the ground or to break apart rocks and minerals. This could lead to new challenges for the energy industry, requiring the development of new technologies and techniques for extracting and processing resources.

While halving the strength of gravity would have significant impacts on our planet, our bodies, and our society, the full range of consequences is not yet fully understood. Further research is needed to better understand the potential impacts of such a change and to ensure that any benefits are realized while minimizing any negative consequences. Whether the benefits of halving gravity would outweigh the costs and challenges remains to be seen, and will likely depend on a wide range of factors, including advances in technology, changes in society and the global economy, and our ability to adapt to a changing world.

Impacts on Wildlife:

A reduction in gravity would also have a significant impact on wildlife, altering the behavior and anatomy of many species. With lighter bodies and more fluid movements, animals would be better able to fly, swim, and move through their environments, potentially leading to new and diverse ecosystems.

However, changes to the food chain and ecosystem could also result in the extinction of certain species, particularly those that rely on specific environmental conditions or behaviors. For example, species that rely on gravity for navigation, such as birds and bats, could experience difficulties finding their way and could be at risk of extinction.

Impacts on Human Health:

The human body would also be greatly affected by a reduction in gravity, with lighter bodies and reduced stress on joints potentially leading to improved health and reduced rates of injury and disease. At the same time, changes to the human body and environment could also lead to new health risks and challenges, such as reduced immunity to disease and increased vulnerability to injury.

In order to fully understand the impacts of reduced gravity on human health, it would be necessary to conduct further research and studies to better understand the effects of reduced gravity on the human body and to develop strategies for minimizing any negative consequences.

The impacts of a reduction in gravity on our planet, our bodies, and our society are complex and wide-ranging, and would likely have both positive and negative consequences. While a reduction in gravity would present new opportunities and challenges, it would also require us to adapt and evolve in order to fully realize its benefits and minimize its risks. Further research and analysis are needed to better understand the full range of impacts and to ensure that any potential benefits are realized while minimizing any negative consequences.

Impacts on Human Settlement:

A reduction in gravity would have significant impacts on human settlement patterns, with lighter structures and reduced stress on foundations potentially leading to new architectural designs and construction methods. At the same time, changes to the environment and weather patterns could also impact human settlements, requiring communities to adapt to new living conditions.

For example, with lighter structures, buildings could be taller and more easily accessible, potentially leading to new opportunities for urban development and the creation of more densely populated cities. At the same time, changes to the water cycle and increased susceptibility to wind and rain could impact the stability and safety of these structures, requiring new strategies for protecting and maintaining them.

Impacts on Transportation:

Transportation would also be impacted by a reduction in gravity, with lighter and more efficient vehicles potentially becoming possible, and new air and water routes becoming available. However, changes to the environment and weather patterns could also impact transportation, requiring new technologies and infrastructure to ensure the safe and efficient movement of people and goods.

For example, lighter vehicles would require less energy to move, potentially reducing the cost of transportation and improving its sustainability. At the same time, changes to the atmosphere and weather patterns could impact the safety and efficiency of air and water transportation, requiring new technologies and infrastructure to adapt to the changing conditions. While a reduction in gravity would present new opportunities and challenges, it would also require us to adapt and evolve in order to fully realize its benefits and minimize its risks. Further research and analysis are needed to better understand the full range of impacts and to ensure that any potential benefits are realized while minimizing any negative consequences.

Impacts on Energy and Resources:

Reduced gravity would also have significant impacts on energy and resource use, as lighter and more efficient systems and technologies become possible. For example, lighter and more efficient vehicles would require less energy to move, potentially reducing the cost of transportation and improving its sustainability. At the same time, changes to the atmosphere and weather patterns could impact the availability and use of renewable energy sources, such as wind and solar power, requiring new strategies for their generation and use.

Impacts on Agriculture:

Agriculture would also be impacted by a reduction in gravity, with changes to soil moisture, temperature, and wind patterns potentially affecting crop yields and the distribution of food resources. In particular, lighter and more fluid movements of water and soil particles could impact the nutrient cycling and availability of plant nutrients, potentially leading to decreased crop yields and food insecurity.

In order to fully understand the impacts of reduced gravity on agriculture, it would be necessary to conduct further research and studies to better understand the effects of reduced gravity on the nutrient cycles and soil dynamics, and to develop strategies for improving food security in the face of these changes. While a reduction in gravity would present new opportunities and challenges, it would also require us to adapt and evolve in order to fully realize its benefits and minimize its risks. Further research and analysis are needed to better understand the full range of impacts and to ensure that any potential benefits are realized while minimizing any negative consequences.

Impacts on Wildlife:

A reduction in gravity would have significant impacts on wildlife, as changes to the physical and environmental conditions could alter the distribution, behavior, and survival of various species. For example, changes to the water cycle and increased susceptibility to wind and rain could impact the survival and migration patterns of many species, as well as their ability to find food and shelter.

At the same time, changes to the physical conditions of the environment could also alter the distribution and behavior of many species, potentially leading to new ecological interactions and the formation of new ecosystems. For example, lighter and more fluid movements of water and soil particles could impact the nutrient cycling and availability of plant nutrients, potentially leading to new food webs and species interactions.

In order to fully understand the impacts of reduced gravity on wildlife, it would be necessary to conduct further research and studies to better understand the effects of reduced gravity on the distribution, behavior, and survival of various species, and to develop strategies for conserving and preserving wildlife in the face of these changes.

Impacts on Global Climate:

A reduction in gravity would also have significant impacts on the global climate, as changes to the atmospheric circulation and the water cycle could alter temperature and precipitation patterns, leading to changes in weather and climate conditions. For example, lighter and more fluid movements of water and air could impact the transport of heat and moisture around the planet, potentially leading to new temperature and precipitation patterns and altering the distribution of ecosystems and biodiversity.

In order to fully understand the impacts of reduced gravity on the global climate, it would be necessary to conduct further research and studies to better understand the effects of reduced gravity on the atmosphere, the water cycle, and the transport of heat and moisture, and to develop strategies for adapting to and mitigating these changes.

The impacts of a reduction in gravity on wildlife and the global climate are complex and wide-ranging, and would have significant impacts on the health and stability of our planet and its ecosystems. While a reduction in gravity would present new opportunities and challenges, it would also require us to adapt and evolve in order to fully realize its benefits and minimize its risks. Further research and analysis are needed to better understand the full range of impacts and to ensure that any potential benefits are realized while minimizing any negative consequences.

Impacts on Human Health:

A halving of gravity would also have profound impacts on human health and well-being. For example, changes to the physical conditions of the environment could impact the musculoskeletal system, potentially leading to changes in posture, balance, and coordination, as well as increased risk of falls and injury.

At the same time, changes to the gravity field could also impact the cardiovascular system, potentially leading to changes in blood pressure and fluid distribution, as well as changes in the functioning of the inner ear, which could impact hearing and balance.

In order to fully understand the impacts of reduced gravity on human health, it would be necessary to conduct further research and studies to better understand the effects of reduced gravity on the musculoskeletal, cardiovascular, and sensory systems, and to develop strategies for mitigating and adapting to these changes.

Impacts on Technology and Infrastructure:

A reduction in gravity would also have significant impacts on technology and infrastructure, as changes to the physical conditions of the environment could impact the design and functionality of buildings, vehicles, and other structures. For example, lighter and more fluid movements of water and air could impact the stability and strength of structures, potentially leading to changes in the design and materials used in construction, as well as the need for new technologies and approaches to engineering and construction.

In order to fully understand the impacts of reduced gravity on technology and infrastructure, it would be necessary to conduct further research and studies to better understand the effects of reduced gravity on the design and functionality of structures, and to develop new technologies and approaches for ensuring the stability and resilience of our infrastructure in the face of these changes.

Impacts on Agriculture:

Agriculture is another sector that would be significantly impacted by a halving of gravity. The reduced gravitational pull would result in changes to the growth patterns of crops and the distribution of soil nutrients, leading to changes in the productivity and yields of crops, as well as changes in the quality and composition of the food we consume.

Additionally, changes to the physical conditions of the environment could also impact the spread of pests and diseases, potentially leading to new outbreaks and new challenges for farmers and food producers. These changes could also impact the distribution and availability of food, leading to new challenges for food security and food distribution systems.

To fully understand the impacts of reduced gravity on agriculture, it would be necessary to conduct further research and studies to better understand the effects of reduced gravity on the growth patterns and yields of crops, as well as the impacts on pest and disease control and food security.

Impacts on Transportation:

The transportation sector would also be significantly impacted by a reduction in gravity. Changes to the physical conditions of the environment would impact the design and functionality of vehicles, potentially leading to changes in the speed, range, and efficiency of vehicles, as well as changes in the infrastructure required to support transportation networks.

Additionally, changes to the physical conditions of the environment could also impact the dynamics of air and water transportation, potentially leading to new opportunities and challenges for these modes of transport.

To fully understand the impacts of reduced gravity on transportation, it would be necessary to conduct further research and studies to better understand the effects of reduced gravity on the design and functionality of vehicles, as well as the impacts on air and water transportation networks.

Impacts on Human Health:

Reduced gravity would also have significant impacts on human health. Changes to the physical conditions of the environment would impact the way our bodies move, potentially leading to changes in our posture, balance, and overall physical health.

Additionally, reduced gravity could also impact the way our bodies process and metabolize food, leading to changes in our nutritional needs and potentially leading to new health challenges. Reduced gravity could also impact the way our bodies deal with physical stress and injury, leading to new challenges for medical professionals and healthcare systems.

To fully understand the impacts of reduced gravity on human health, it would be necessary to conduct further research and studies to better understand the effects of reduced gravity on our physical and physiological health, as well as the impacts on healthcare systems and medical practices.

Impacts on Architecture and Construction:

A reduction in gravity would also impact the architecture and construction sectors, as the reduced gravitational pull would require new designs and construction techniques to ensure the safety and stability of buildings and infrastructure.

Changes to the physical conditions of the environment could also impact the way buildings and structures are used, leading to new challenges for building codes, regulations, and standards. Additionally, reduced gravity could impact the materials and techniques used in construction, leading to new challenges for construction and engineering professionals.

To fully understand the impacts of reduced gravity on architecture and construction, it would be necessary to conduct further research and studies to better understand the effects of reduced gravity on building design, construction techniques, and the overall safety and stability of buildings and infrastructure.

Impacts on Energy and Power Generation:

Reduced gravity would also have significant impacts on the energy and power generation sectors. Changes to the physical conditions of the environment could impact the way energy is generated and distributed, potentially leading to changes in the efficiency and effectiveness of energy generation and distribution systems.

Additionally, changes to the physical conditions of the environment could also impact the way we use energy, potentially leading to changes in energy consumption patterns and energy demand. This could result in new challenges for energy producers and energy grid operators, as they would need to adapt to changing conditions and find new ways to meet energy demand.

To fully understand the impacts of reduced gravity on energy and power generation, it would be necessary to conduct further research and studies to better understand the effects of reduced gravity on energy generation and distribution systems, as well as the impacts on energy consumption patterns and energy demand.

Impacts on Space Exploration and Technology:

Reduced gravity would also have significant impacts on space exploration and technology. Changes to the physical conditions of the environment could impact the way we explore and use space, potentially leading to new challenges and opportunities for space exploration and technology.

Reduced gravity could impact the design and functionality of spacecraft, leading to new challenges for space engineers and designers. Additionally, reduced gravity could impact the way we use satellites and other space-based technologies, potentially leading to new challenges for satellite operators and other stakeholders in the space industry.

To fully understand the impacts of reduced gravity on space exploration and technology, it would be necessary to conduct further research and studies to better understand the effects of reduced gravity on spacecraft design and functionality, as well as the impacts on satellite operations and other aspects of the space industry.

Impacts on Agriculture and Food Production:

The reduced gravitational pull would also impact the agriculture and food production sectors. Changes to the physical conditions of the environment could impact the way plants grow and develop, potentially leading to changes in crop yields and quality.

Additionally, changes to the physical conditions of the environment could also impact the way animals and insects interact with plants, potentially leading to changes in pest and disease patterns and other ecological factors. This could result in new challenges for farmers, as they would need to adapt to changing conditions and find new ways to maintain healthy and productive crops.

To fully understand the impacts of reduced gravity on agriculture and food production, it would be necessary to conduct further research and studies to better understand the effects of reduced gravity on plant growth and development, as well as the impacts on pest and disease patterns and other ecological factors.

Impacts on Climate and Weather:

Reduced gravity would also have impacts on climate and weather patterns. Changes to the physical conditions of the environment could impact the way air and water circulate, potentially leading to changes in global weather patterns and the distribution of precipitation.

Additionally, changes to the physical conditions of the environment could also impact the way heat is absorbed and transferred, potentially leading to changes in global temperature patterns and the overall energy balance of the planet.

To fully understand the impacts of reduced gravity on climate and weather, it would be necessary to conduct further research and studies to better understand the effects of reduced gravity on air and water circulation, as well as the impacts on heat transfer and the overall energy balance of the planet.

Impacts on Space Exploration:

Reduced gravity would also have a significant impact on space exploration. The reduced gravitational pull would make it easier for spacecraft to escape Earth's gravitational pull and travel to other celestial bodies, potentially making space exploration more feasible and cost-effective.

However, reduced gravity would also have implications for the physical conditions that astronauts would experience during space travel and on other celestial bodies. For example, changes in the gravitational pull could impact the way fluids circulate in the human body, potentially leading to changes in human physiology and health.

To fully understand the impacts of reduced gravity on space exploration, it would be necessary to conduct further research and studies to better understand the effects of reduced gravity on human physiology and health, as well as the impacts on spacecraft design and operations.

Impacts on Infrastructure:

Reduced gravity would also have impacts on infrastructure, as it would alter the forces that buildings and other structures are exposed to. For example, changes to the gravitational pull could impact the way buildings and bridges are designed, constructed, and maintained, potentially leading to changes in building codes and standards.

Additionally, changes to the gravitational pull could also impact the way transportation systems are designed and operated, potentially leading to changes in the design and operation of trains, cars, and airplanes.

To fully understand the impacts of reduced gravity on infrastructure, it would be necessary to conduct further research and studies to better understand the effects of reduced gravity on building design and construction, as well as the impacts on transportation systems.

In conclusion, a halving of gravity would have far-reaching and profound impacts on virtually every aspect of our lives. From the way we grow food, to the way we build and operate our transportation systems, the reduced gravitational pull would necessitate a significant rethinking of the way we live and work. The impacts on human physiology and health would also require further study, to fully understand the implications of reduced gravity on human life. Ultimately, a halving of gravity would represent a major shift in the conditions of our world, with both opportunities for innovation and new challenges to be addressed. While the halving of gravity may seem like a far-fetched scenario, it is important to consider the potential impacts of such a change and to be prepared to respond and adapt to these changes if they were to occur.

CHAPTER THREE

WHAT WOULD HAPPEN IF THE MOON WERE SUDDENLY REMOVED FROM ITS ORBIT?

Introduction:

The moon is one of the most significant natural satellites in our solar system, having a profound impact on the Earth and its inhabitants. From influencing ocean tides to providing a stable gravitational force, the moon plays a critical role in maintaining the stability of our planet. But what would happen if the moon were suddenly removed from its orbit? This chapter will examine the potential consequences of such an event.

Impacts on the Earth's Rotation:

One of the most significant impacts of the removal of the moon from its orbit would be changes to the Earth's rotation. The moon's gravitational pull helps to stabilize the Earth's axis, preventing it from wobbling excessively. Without the moon, the Earth's axis would become much less stable, potentially leading to more extreme variations in climate and weather patterns.

Impacts on Ocean Tides:

The moon's gravitational pull is also responsible for the Earth's ocean tides, which play a crucial role in the world's ecosystems. The removal of the moon from its orbit would result in a significant decrease in the size and frequency of ocean tides, potentially disrupting the delicate balance of ocean ecosystems and affecting the survival of marine species.

Impacts on the Earth's Magnetic Field:

The moon's gravitational pull also helps to maintain the Earth's magnetic field, which protects the planet from harmful solar and cosmic radiation. Without the moon, the Earth's magnetic field would become weaker, potentially leading to an increase in the amount of harmful radiation that reaches the planet's surface. This could have significant impacts on human health, as well as the health of other species.

Impacts on Climate and Weather Patterns:

The removal of the moon from its orbit could also lead to changes in the Earth's climate and weather patterns. The moon helps to regulate the Earth's axial tilt, which has a significant impact on the distribution of sunlight across the planet's surface. Without the moon, the axial tilt would become more unstable, potentially leading to changes in climate and weather patterns.

Impacts on the Earth's Rotation:

One of the most significant impacts of the removal of the moon from its orbit would be changes to the Earth's rotation. The moon's gravitational pull helps to stabilize the Earth's axis, preventing it from wobbling excessively. Without the moon, the Earth's axis would become much less stable, potentially leading to more extreme variations in climate and weather patterns.

Impacts on Ocean Tides:

The moon's gravitational pull is also responsible for the Earth's ocean tides, which play a crucial role in the world's ecosystems. The removal of the moon from its orbit would result in a significant decrease in the size and frequency of ocean tides, potentially disrupting the delicate balance of ocean ecosystems and affecting the survival of marine species.

Impacts on the Earth's Magnetic Field:

The moon's gravitational pull also helps to maintain the Earth's magnetic field, which protects the planet from harmful solar and cosmic radiation. Without the moon, the Earth's magnetic field would become weaker, potentially leading to an increase in the amount of harmful radiation that reaches the planet's surface. This could have significant impacts on human health, as well as the health of other species.

Impacts on Climate and Weather Patterns:

The removal of the moon from its orbit could also lead to changes in the Earth's climate and weather patterns. The moon helps to regulate the Earth's axial tilt, which has a significant impact on the distribution of sunlight across the planet's surface. Without the moon, the axial tilt would become more unstable, potentially leading to changes in climate and weather patterns.

Impacts on Earth's Orbital Path:

Another significant impact of the removal of the moon from its orbit would be changes to the Earth's orbital path. The moon's gravitational pull helps to keep the Earth in its current orbital path, preventing it from straying too far from the sun. Without the moon's gravitational pull, the Earth's orbital path could become more unstable, potentially leading to significant changes in climate, weather patterns, and the amount of solar radiation that reaches the planet's surface.

Impacts on Natural Satellites:

The removal of the moon from its orbit could also have impacts on other natural satellites in the Earth's system. For example, the moon's gravitational pull helps to stabilize the orbits of smaller satellites, such as asteroids and comets, preventing them from colliding with the Earth. Without the moon, these smaller satellites would become more unstable, potentially increasing the risk of impact events.

Impacts on Human Civilization:

The removal of the moon from its orbit would also have significant impacts on human civilization. The changes in the Earth's climate, weather patterns, and magnetic field, as well as the increased risk of impact events from smaller satellites, could all have disastrous consequences for human populations. Additionally, the changes in the Earth's rotation and orbital path could make it difficult for humans to accurately predict and prepare for future events.

Impacts on Tides:

The moon's gravitational pull is responsible for the tides on Earth, causing a rise and fall of sea levels on a daily basis. Without the moon, the tides would cease to exist, leading to significant impacts on coastal ecosystems and communities. Coastal areas that rely on the tides to bring in nutrients and oxygen to support their ecosystems would be severely affected. Additionally, many human activities, such as fishing, shipping, and coastal tourism, would also be negatively impacted by the absence of tides.

Impacts on Earth's Axial Tilt:

The moon also plays a role in regulating the Earth's axial tilt, which affects the planet's climate and weather patterns. The moon's gravitational pull helps to keep the Earth's axis tilted at a stable angle, preventing the planet from wobbling too much. Without the moon, the Earth's axial tilt could become more unstable, leading to significant changes in the planet's climate and weather patterns.

Impacts on Earth's Rotation:

The moon's gravitational pull also affects the Earth's rotation. The moon slows down the Earth's rotation over time, which helps to keep the planet's day and night cycle stable. Without the moon, the Earth's rotation could speed up, potentially leading to changes in the length of the day and night.

Impacts on Astronomy:

The removal of the moon from its orbit would have significant impacts on astronomy and space exploration. The moon is used as a reference point for many astronomical observations, and its absence could make it more difficult to study the stars, planets, and other celestial bodies. Additionally, the moon has been used as a stepping stone for human space exploration, and its absence could impact future plans for space missions.

Effects on Earth's Geology:

The moon's gravitational pull has a significant effect on Earth's geology. The moon's gravitational pull causes the ocean tides, which can erode the coastlines over time. The absence of the moon's gravitational pull would stop this process, potentially leading to changes in the shape of the coastlines. Additionally, the moon has also been credited with stabilizing the Earth's axial tilt, which affects the planet's climate. The absence of the moon could cause the Earth's axial tilt to become unstable, leading to changes in the planet's climate and weather patterns.

Effects on Artificial Satellites:

Artificial satellites orbiting the Earth rely on the moon's gravitational pull to maintain their orbits. The absence of the moon could disrupt the orbits of these satellites, potentially causing them to fall back to Earth. This would have significant impacts on communication, navigation, and weather prediction, which rely on these satellites to provide accurate data and services.

Effects on Life on Earth:

The absence of the moon would also have significant impacts on life on Earth. The moon's gravitational pull affects the tides, which provide nutrients and oxygen to coastal ecosystems. Without the moon, these ecosystems would be severely impacted, potentially leading to changes in the types of species that can survive in these areas. Additionally, the absence of the moon could cause changes in the Earth's climate and weather patterns, which could affect crops, wildlife, and human populations.

Effects on Mythology and Culture:

The absence of the moon would also have cultural and mythological impacts. The moon has played a role in many cultures and religions, serving as a symbol of the night, a celestial body to be worshipped, and a marker of time. The absence of the moon could change the way that people view the night sky and their place in the world.

Impact on Lunar Eclipses:

Lunar eclipses occur when the moon passes through the Earth's shadow. These events are significant for both scientific and cultural reasons, as they provide information about the Earth's atmosphere and have been used for centuries as a means of predicting eclipses and other astronomical events. The absence of the moon would eliminate the possibility of lunar eclipses, which could have significant impacts on astronomical research and the study of the Earth's atmosphere.

Impact on Tides:

The moon's gravitational pull is responsible for the rise and fall of the tides on Earth. This is a critical component of many coastal ecosystems, as the tides bring in nutrients and oxygen, which support the growth of plants and animals. Without the moon, tides would cease to exist, leading to changes in the types of species that can survive in these areas. This could have a significant impact on the world's coastal ecosystems, including wetlands, estuaries, and coral reefs.

Impact on Earth's Rotation:

The moon's gravitational pull has also been credited with slowing down the Earth's rotation over time. This has helped to stabilize the planet's axial tilt, which affects the planet's climate and weather patterns. The absence of the moon could cause the Earth's rotation to speed up, leading to changes in the planet's climate and weather patterns. This could have a significant impact on crops, wildlife, and human populations, as well as the stability of the planet's climate and ecosystems.

Impact on the Space Industry:

The absence of the moon could have significant impacts on the space industry. The moon has long been a target for human exploration, both as a scientific research platform and as a potential resource for minerals and other materials. The absence of the moon would eliminate the possibility of human exploration and the development of the moon as a resource. This could have significant impacts on the future of the space industry and the exploration of space.

In addition to the impacts on the Earth's tides and ocean currents, the loss of the moon would also have a significant effect on the planet's axial tilt. The moon has a stabilizing effect on the Earth's axial tilt, which keeps it within a range of about 22.1 to 24.5 degrees. Without the moon, the axial tilt would become unstable and could vary wildly, leading to severe changes in climate patterns. The Earth's axial tilt is responsible for the changing of seasons, and drastic changes in its tilt could result in extreme weather patterns and temperature swings.

The moon also has an effect on the Earth's magnetic field, which protects the planet from harmful solar and cosmic radiation. The moon's gravitational pull helps to maintain the shape of the Earth's magnetic field, and without it, the magnetic field could become distorted and weakened, leading to increased exposure to harmful radiation.

The absence of the moon would also have a profound impact on the planet's geological processes. The moon's gravitational pull affects the Earth's plate tectonics, which are responsible for the formation of mountains, earthquakes, and volcanic eruptions. Without the moon, plate tectonic processes could become destabilized, leading to more frequent and intense seismic activity.

The loss of the moon would also have an impact on our planet's orbit and rotation. The moon's gravitational pull helps to regulate the Earth's orbit around the sun and slows down its rotation. Without the moon, the Earth's rotation would speed up and its orbit could become unstable, leading to significant changes in the length of the day and the timing of the seasons. This could have severe consequences for agriculture, as crops are finely tuned to specific daylight hours and seasonal changes.

In addition, the moon is believed to have played a critical role in the evolution of life on Earth. It has helped to regulate the Earth's axial tilt, which has allowed for a stable and predictable climate that has allowed life to flourish. The loss of the moon could have resulted in a much more chaotic and unstable climate, making it much harder for life to evolve and thrive.

The absence of the moon would have a significant impact on our tides and ocean currents. The moon's gravitational pull causes the tides, and without it, tides would become much less predictable and could lead to severe coastal flooding. In addition, ocean currents could become destabilized, leading to changes in marine ecosystems and the distribution of ocean species.

The removal of the moon would also have an impact on our view of the night sky. The moon is one of the brightest objects in the sky and its absence would result in a much darker and less visible night sky. This could have a significant impact on our sense of place and connection to the universe.

Additionally, without the moon's gravitational pull, tides would be affected and coastlines could experience severe erosion. The tides play a crucial role in shaping coastlines, and without the moon, they would not be as strong or predictable. This could result in increased coastal flooding and erosion, leading to significant damage to infrastructure and loss of property.

Another significant impact of the moon's disappearance would be on the Earth's axial tilt. The moon helps stabilize the Earth's axial tilt, preventing it from wobbling too much. If the moon were suddenly removed, the Earth's axial tilt would become unstable, leading to significant changes in the planet's climate. This could result in irregular weather patterns, increased natural disasters, and even mass extinction events.

The removal of the moon would have a profound impact on human society. Navigation and timekeeping have relied on the moon for centuries, and without it, it would be difficult to determine precise locations and times. This could disrupt transportation, communication, and commerce, leading to significant economic and social consequences. Additionally, the moon's absence could impact human culture, as it has long been a source of inspiration and wonder for people all over the world.

If the moon were suddenly removed from its orbit, the impact on the Earth and human society would be profound. From changes to the Earth's orbit and tides to the loss of a fundamental tool for navigation and timekeeping, the disappearance of the moon would have far-reaching and long-lasting consequences.

CHAPTER FOUR

HOW COULD WE POTENTIALLY TERRAFORM ANOTHER PLANET TO SUPPORT HUMAN LIFE?

Introduction:

Terraforming refers to the process of modifying the environment of a celestial body to make it more hospitable to human life. While there have been numerous discussions and studies regarding the possibility of terraforming Mars, the red planet is not the only candidate for terraforming. In this chapter, we will explore the potential for terraforming other planets and how this could be accomplished.

Body:

Identifying suitable planets: The first step in terraforming a planet is to identify a planet that is suitable for this process. Some of the key factors that need to be considered include the planet's size, atmosphere, and distance from its star. A planet with a similar size and atmosphere to Earth would be ideal, but finding such a planet that is close enough to a star to provide the necessary energy would be challenging.

Modifying the atmosphere: A planet's atmosphere plays a critical role in determining its suitability for human life. A terraformed planet would need to have an atmosphere that is thick enough to protect against harmful cosmic radiation and provide enough pressure for humans to breathe. It would also need to contain the right balance of gases, such as oxygen, to support human life. If the target planet does not have a suitable atmosphere, it would need to be created through artificial means.

Creating a magnetic field: A magnetic field is essential for protecting a planet's atmosphere and surface from harmful cosmic radiation. If the target planet does not have a magnetic field, one would need to be created. This could be accomplished by launching a large, magnetized object into orbit around the planet or by using other artificial means.

Regulating the temperature: The temperature on the surface of a planet can play a crucial role in determining its suitability for human life. A planet that is too hot or too cold would not be ideal for human habitation. To regulate the temperature, various methods could be employed, such as using reflective materials to deflect heat or launching artificial satellites to regulate the planet's temperature.

Introducing life: To make a planet truly hospitable to human life, it would be necessary to introduce various forms of life to the planet. This could include plants, animals, and microorganisms. This would help to create a stable ecosystem and provide the necessary resources to support human life.

Terraforming another planet would require addressing several challenges in order to create a suitable environment for human life. One of the first steps would be to regulate the planet's temperature so that it can support liquid water, which is essential for life as we know it. This can be achieved by several means, including introducing greenhouse gases into the planet's atmosphere or modifying the planet's orbit so that it is closer to its sun.

Another important factor is atmospheric pressure, which must be in a range that allows for the retention of gases and liquids. This would likely require the introduction of nitrogen, oxygen, and other gases into the atmosphere, in order to increase the atmospheric pressure. It may also be necessary to protect the planet from harmful solar and cosmic radiation, which could be done by creating a magnetic field or by adding a thick atmosphere.

In order to support human life, a planet must also have a stable and solid surface, with enough gravity to prevent objects from floating away. This would likely involve the creation of a strong enough magnetic field to protect against solar wind, which can strip away the atmosphere and make a planet uninhabitable.

In addition to these basic requirements, terraforming another planet would also require the introduction of a source of food and water, as well as a source of energy. This could be achieved through the creation of an ecosystem that includes plants and animals, or by importing resources from other planets or systems.

It will be important to consider the long-term sustainability of the terraformed planet, including the need for continued maintenance and monitoring to ensure that the environment remains suitable for human life. This will require significant investment in technology, infrastructure, and research, as well as a commitment from humanity to protect and preserve the new world for future generations.

One potential method of terraforming another planet would be to modify its atmosphere to one that is more similar to Earth's. This could be done by introducing gases that would warm the planet, such as carbon dioxide or methane, or by introducing oxygen to create a breathable atmosphere. Another potential method of terraforming a planet would be to modify its surface to be more similar to Earth's, such as by building artificial structures and modifying the soil. This could potentially involve the use of large-scale terraforming machinery, such as robotic earthmovers, to modify the landscape and build infrastructure.

Another important factor in terraforming a planet is the need for a stable and predictable climate. This could be achieved by manipulating the planet's orbit and axial tilt, or by introducing a secondary satellite to stabilize its orbit. Additionally, the presence of liquid water is crucial for the development of life on a planet, so it may be necessary to bring water to the planet or to introduce other sources of moisture.

There are also many challenges that would need to be addressed in order to successfully terraform a planet. For example, the planet's gravity and magnetic field would need to be studied in order to determine whether or not it would be able to support human life. The planet would also need to have a stable interior, without any active volcanic activity or tectonic plates that could cause earthquakes or other disasters. In addition, the planet would need to be free of any harmful radiations or other environmental hazards that could harm human health.

Ultimately, terraforming a planet is a complex and challenging process that would require a great deal of scientific and technological expertise, as well as significant resources. However, if successful, it would provide an exciting new opportunity for humanity to expand its reach into the cosmos and to establish new colonies on other worlds.

Terraforming another planet to support human life would require significant engineering and technology advances. Some of the major steps required for terraforming a planet include:

Climate Modification: The planet's climate would have to be modified to make it hospitable for human life. This could involve altering the planet's atmospheric composition, increasing the atmospheric pressure, and regulating the temperature.

Creation of a Magnetic Field: A strong magnetic field would have to be created to protect the planet from harmful solar and cosmic radiation.

Provision of Water: A source of water would have to be established, either by bringing water from other sources or by creating an artificial water cycle. This could involve introducing ice or other water-rich materials to the planet's surface, or manipulating the planet's atmosphere to promote rainfall.

Generation of Breathable Atmosphere: The planet's atmosphere would have to be composed of gases that are safe and suitable for human respiration, such as nitrogen and oxygen. This could be achieved by introducing these gases to the planet's atmosphere, or by modifying the existing atmosphere to make it more breathable.

Soil Enhancement: The soil on the planet would need to be made suitable for growing crops and sustaining plant life, which is essential for supporting human life. This could be done by adding nutrients and minerals to the soil, or by using genetic engineering to create crops that are better suited to the planet's soil.

Introduction of Microorganisms: A diverse and thriving ecosystem of microorganisms is necessary for maintaining the health and balance of the planet's environment. This could be achieved by introducing beneficial microorganisms, or by modifying the existing microorganisms to better support the planet's environment.

Climate Control: The planet's climate would need to be controlled and stabilized to create a stable and hospitable environment for human life. This could be done by using artificial means, such as creating an artificial magnetic field to protect against solar radiation, or by modifying the planet's atmosphere to regulate its temperature.

Terraforming a planet to support human life involves a number of complex and interrelated processes. One of the first steps in terraforming a planet is to create a stable and sustainable atmosphere. This typically involves adding oxygen and other essential gases to the planet's atmosphere, as well as increasing the pressure and temperature to levels that are hospitable for human life.

Another key aspect of terraforming a planet is to modify the surface conditions so that they are more hospitable for human life. This might involve manipulating the planet's climate to create more temperate conditions, or using techniques such as landscape engineering to create a more varied and livable landscape.

One of the main challenges in terraforming a planet is to ensure that the changes being made to the planet's environment do not negatively impact the planet's existing ecosystem. This requires a careful and deliberate approach to terraforming, taking into account the complex interplay between different environmental factors, such as temperature, pressure, and atmospheric composition.

In order to terraform a planet successfully, it is also important to have a deep understanding of the planet's geology, biology, and climate. This will help to identify any potential challenges or limitations that may arise during the terraforming process, and to develop strategies to overcome them.

Another important factor to consider when terraforming a planet is the availability of resources. In order to carry out the necessary modifications to the planet's environment, significant amounts of resources will be required, including energy, materials, and specialized equipment. These resources will need to be sourced from elsewhere in the solar system, or from beyond, making terraforming a planet a complex and challenging process that requires significant investment and expertise.

One possible approach to terraforming another planet would be to modify its atmosphere. This could involve introducing gases such as oxygen and nitrogen, which are essential for human survival, as well as increasing the atmospheric pressure to create a livable environment. Another option could be to modify the planet's temperature, which could be achieved by positioning satellites in orbit to reflect sunlight, or by installing massive sunshades to block the sun's rays.

Another aspect of terraforming that would need to be addressed is the planet's water cycle. This could be achieved by creating a new water cycle by transporting ice or water from other locations in the solar system, or by developing new technologies to extract water from the planet's surface.

In order to support human life, the planet's magnetic field would also need to be strengthened. This could be achieved by installing massive electromagnets to create an artificial magnetic field, or by launching satellites equipped with magnetic generators into orbit.

Additionally, new technologies would need to be developed to support agriculture and food production. This could involve creating new strains of crops that are able to withstand the harsh conditions of the new planet, or developing hydroponic and aeroponic farming methods that can grow crops in a controlled environment.

It would be important to address any potential threats to human health and safety. This could involve creating new medical technologies to treat illnesses and injuries, or developing systems to protect against radiation and other dangerous environmental factors.

Terraforming a planet involves making significant changes to the planet's environment to make it habitable for humans. There are a number of different approaches to terraforming that have been proposed, and the methods used will depend on the specific planet being targeted for terraforming.

One of the key factors to consider when terraforming a planet is the presence of water. If a planet has water, it can be a good candidate for terraforming because water is a vital resource for human life. However, if a planet does not have water, it may not be feasible to terraform it.

Another factor that must be considered when terraforming a planet is the planet's atmosphere. The atmosphere must be capable of supporting human life, which requires the presence of breathable air. This means that the atmosphere must contain a mix of gases that are similar to the mix of gases found on Earth.

In order to terraform a planet, it is also important to have a source of energy. This can be provided by the sun, which can be harnessed using solar panels. Alternatively, nuclear power could be used as a source of energy.

One of the most important aspects of terraforming a planet is the creation of a biosphere. This involves introducing life to the planet, which can help to establish a sustainable ecosystem. This can be done by introducing microbes, plants, and animals that are adapted to living in harsh environments.

There are many potential challenges to terraforming another planet. One of the biggest challenges is creating a suitable atmosphere for human life. Terraforming requires a change in atmospheric composition, pressure, and temperature, which is a difficult and long-term process. The planet's atmosphere must be able to support life by providing the necessary elements such as nitrogen, oxygen, and carbon dioxide. Additionally, a planet's atmosphere must also be able to protect life from harmful radiation, such as ultraviolet radiation from the sun.

Another challenge in terraforming is creating a stable climate. A stable climate is crucial for supporting life and allowing crops to grow. For example, a terraformed planet might need to have a strong magnetic field to protect against solar winds and cosmic radiation, which can disrupt the climate and create storms. Additionally, the planet's axial tilt and orbit must be stabilized to ensure a consistent climate.

Terraforming also requires a change in the planet's surface and geography. For example, a planet might need to have oceans and continents to create a diverse and hospitable environment for life. This could be done through the introduction of water and other elements such as carbon, nitrogen, and phosphorus to the planet's surface. Additionally, the planet's surface must be able to support life by having the right chemical composition and mineral resources.

Terraforming will require a significant investment in resources, technology, and time. It will require a large team of scientists, engineers, and other experts, as well as a significant amount of funding to support their research and development efforts. Additionally, terraforming will take many years, even decades or centuries, to accomplish.

While terraforming another planet is a complex and challenging process, it is also a fascinating area of study with the potential to dramatically change our understanding of the universe and our place in it.

In conclusion, terraforming another planet to support human life is a complex and challenging task that would require extensive scientific and technological advances. There are various methods and technologies that have been proposed to make this a reality, including introducing Earth-like environments, modifying the planet's atmosphere, and engineering new ecosystems. However, significant research and development must be carried out to determine the feasibility and sustainability of these methods. Additionally, ethical and moral considerations must be taken into account, such as the potential impact on any existing extraterrestrial life forms. Ultimately, the success of terraforming another planet will depend on the combined efforts of scientists, engineers, and policymakers, working together to create a new world that is safe, hospitable, and sustainable for humanity.

CHAPTER FIVE

How would the world be different if humans had never evolved?

This chapter aims to explore the impact that the absence of human beings would have on the world, if they had never evolved. Through the examination of various scientific disciplines, including biology, ecology, and geology, we will attempt to paint a picture of what the planet would look like in a hypothetical scenario where humans never existed. The chapter argues that the absence of humans would have resulted in significant changes in the composition of ecosystems and the course of geological processes, which in turn would have greatly impacted the overall state of the planet.

Introduction:

Human beings are unique in many ways, with our ability to communicate, think, and create being among the most notable. It is therefore interesting to consider what the world might be like if humans had never evolved. In this chapter, we will explore the impact that the absence of humans would have on the world, from an ecological and geological perspective.

Impact on Ecosystems:

In the absence of humans, many species that were driven to extinction by human activities would still be present on the planet. For example, the woolly mammoth, which became extinct approximately 4,000 years ago, would still be roaming the earth. The absence of human activities, such as hunting and habitat destruction, would also have allowed other threatened species, such as the Bengal tiger and the African elephant, to flourish.

The composition of ecosystems would also be vastly different in the absence of humans. For example, in areas where humans have been heavily involved in agriculture, forests would have likely re-grown and the balance between different species of plants and animals would have been re-established. On the other hand, in areas where humans have caused extensive damage through activities like deforestation, new ecosystems would have developed.

Impact on Geological Processes:

The absence of human activities would have resulted in significant changes in geological processes as well. For example, without human-caused pollution, the atmosphere would likely be much cleaner and have a different composition. Similarly, the absence of human activities, such as dam building, would result in a more natural flow of rivers and streams, leading to different patterns of erosion and sedimentation.

The absence of human activities, such as mining, would result in different patterns of mineral deposits, as geological processes would continue uninterrupted. Additionally, the absence of human activities, such as urbanization, would result in a different distribution of earthquakes, as the removal of weight from certain areas would not occur.

Impact on Ecosystems:

In the absence of human activities, many species that were driven to extinction would still exist on the planet. For instance, the woolly mammoth, which became extinct approximately 4,000 years ago, would still roam the earth, and the balance between different species of plants and animals would be re-established. In areas where humans have been involved in agriculture, forests would have likely re-grown, and in areas where humans have caused extensive damage, such as deforestation, new ecosystems would have developed.

The composition of ecosystems would also change in the absence of humans. Human activities, such as hunting and habitat destruction, have greatly impacted the balance of species in many areas, and the absence of these activities would allow threatened species, such as the Bengal tiger and the African elephant, to flourish. Additionally, the introduction of non-native species, which often occurs due to human activities, would not take place, resulting in different species distributions.

Impact on Geological Processes:

The absence of human activities would also result in changes in geological processes. Human-caused pollution, such as industrial waste and plastic, would not exist, leading to a cleaner atmosphere with a different composition. The absence of human activities, such as dam building and mining, would result in a more natural flow of rivers and streams and different patterns of erosion and sedimentation. The absence of urbanization would also result in a different distribution of earthquakes, as the removal of weight from certain areas would not occur.

Human activities have greatly impacted the planet's natural processes, and the absence of these activities would lead to a vastly different world. The impact of human activities, such as deforestation and pollution, often goes unnoticed, but it is clear that humans have a profound impact on the planet and its processes.

Impact on Biodiversity:

Biodiversity, the variety of species and ecosystems on the planet, would also be greatly impacted by the absence of humans. The extinction of species due to human activities, such as hunting and habitat destruction, would not take place, leading to a greater variety of species and a more diverse range of ecosystems. In addition, the introduction of non-native species, which often leads to the decline of native species, would not occur.

Without human activities, such as agriculture and urbanization, large areas of land that are currently used for these purposes would revert back to their natural state, leading to the re-establishment of ecosystems and the growth of forests. This, in turn, would lead to an increase in biodiversity and a greater variety of species.

Impact on Climate:

Without human activities, the world's climate would be vastly different. Human activities, such as deforestation, urbanization, and the burning of fossil fuels, have greatly impacted the Earth's atmosphere, leading to an increase in greenhouse gases and global warming. In the absence of these activities, the Earth's climate would likely be much cooler, and the pattern of seasons and weather events would be different.

For example, without human-caused deforestation, more forests would exist, leading to greater absorption of carbon dioxide from the atmosphere, which would reduce the greenhouse effect and cool the planet. Furthermore, without human activities that release greenhouse gases into the atmosphere, such as the burning of fossil fuels, the amount of these gases in the atmosphere would decrease, leading to a cooler climate.

Impact on Evolution:

The absence of human activities would also result in changes to the course of evolution. Evolution, the process by which species change over time, is often driven by environmental factors, such as changes in climate, the introduction of new species, and the extinction of others. In the absence of human activities, these factors would be different, leading to different patterns of evolution.

For example, without human-caused extinction, species that are currently endangered or threatened would not become extinct, and their evolutionary pathways would continue. On the other hand, without human activities that introduce new species, such as the transport of species through trade and commerce, the distribution of species and the formation of new ecosystems would be different.

Impact on Geography:

The absence of human activities would also result in changes to the world's geography. Human activities, such as dam building, urbanization, and deforestation, have greatly impacted the Earth's surface, leading to changes in the flow of rivers and streams, the formation of new land masses, and the loss of forests. In the absence of these activities, the Earth's surface would likely be much different, with different patterns of erosion, sedimentation, and the formation of land masses.

For example, without human-caused dam building, the flow of rivers and streams would be more natural, leading to different patterns of erosion and sedimentation. Additionally, without human activities that cause deforestation, such as agriculture and urbanization, forests would re-grow, leading to a different distribution of land masses. The absence of humans would result in significant changes to the world, including changes to the Earth's climate, evolution, and geography. These changes would result in a vastly different world, with different species, ecosystems, and geological processes. It is clear that humans have a profound impact on the planet, and that our actions must be guided by a desire to preserve the delicate balance of the natural world.

Impact on Animal Populations:

The absence of human activities would result in significant changes to the populations of animals around the world. Human activities, such as hunting, habitat destruction, and the introduction of non-native species, have greatly impacted animal populations, leading to declines in some species and the extinction of others. In the absence of these activities, animal populations would likely be much different, with different patterns of distribution and abundance.

For example, without human-caused habitat destruction, animal populations would have more suitable habitats, leading to greater abundance and diversity of species. Furthermore, without human activities that introduce non-native species, such as the transportation of species through trade and commerce, native species would not be threatened by the competition and predation of introduced species.

Impact on Plant Populations:

The absence of human activities would also result in changes to the populations of plants around the world. Human activities, such as agriculture, urbanization, and deforestation, have greatly impacted plant populations, leading to declines in some species and the extinction of others. In the absence of these activities, plant populations would likely be much different, with different patterns of distribution and abundance.

For example, without human-caused deforestation, plant populations would have more suitable habitats, leading to greater abundance and diversity of species. Additionally, without human activities that cause soil degradation, such as agriculture and urbanization, soil would be healthier, leading to greater productivity and diversity of plant species.

Impact on Ecosystems:

The absence of human activities would result in significant changes to the ecosystems of the world. Ecosystems are complex networks of interactions between species, including predator-prey relationships, competition for resources, and symbiotic relationships. Human activities, such as habitat destruction, the introduction of non-native species, and the disruption of natural processes, have greatly impacted ecosystems, leading to declines in some species and the extinction of others. In the absence of these activities, ecosystems would likely be much different, with different patterns of species interactions and functioning.

For example, without human-caused habitat destruction, ecosystems would have more suitable habitats, leading to greater abundance and diversity of species.

Furthermore, without human activities that introduce non-native species, ecosystems would not be threatened by the competition and predation of introduced species. Additionally, without human activities that disrupt natural processes, such as the damming of rivers, ecosystems would function more naturally, with more stable and diverse populations of species.

Impact on Biodiversity:

The absence of human activities would result in significant changes to the biodiversity of the world. Biodiversity, the variety of species and ecosystems, is a crucial aspect of the health and functioning of the planet. Human activities, such as habitat destruction, the introduction of non-native species, and the exploitation of species for commercial purposes, have greatly impacted biodiversity, leading to declines in some species and the extinction of others. In the absence of these activities, biodiversity would likely be much greater, with more species and ecosystems.

For example, without human-caused habitat destruction, there would be more suitable habitats for species, leading to greater abundance and diversity of species. Furthermore, without human activities that introduce non-native species, ecosystems would not be threatened by the competition and predation of introduced species, leading to greater stability and diversity of species. Additionally, without human activities that exploit species for commercial purposes, such as fishing and hunting, species populations would be more abundant, leading to greater biodiversity.

Impact on Natural Processes:

The absence of human activities would also result in changes to the natural processes of the world. Natural processes, such as the water cycle, the carbon cycle, and the nutrient cycles, are crucial for the functioning of the planet. Human activities, such as deforestation, urbanization, and the burning of fossil fuels, have greatly impacted these processes, leading to changes in the balance of the Earth's systems. In the absence of these activities, the natural processes would likely be more stable, with more consistent patterns of function.

For example, without human-caused deforestation, the water cycle would be more stable, with less runoff and greater retention of water in the landscape. Additionally, without human activities that release greenhouse gases into the atmosphere, such as the burning of fossil fuels, the carbon cycle would be more balanced, with less carbon dioxide in the atmosphere and greater uptake of carbon by vegetation. Furthermore, without human activities that disrupt nutrient cycles, such as agriculture and urbanization, nutrient cycles would be more stable, with more efficient recycling of nutrients in the landscape.

Impact on Geography:

The absence of humans would result in significant changes to the geography of the world. Human activities, such as urbanization, deforestation, and the construction of dams and other infrastructure, have greatly impacted the geography of the world, leading to changes in land use patterns, the formation of urban centers, and the alteration of natural landscapes. In the absence of these activities, the geography of the world would likely be vastly different.

For example, without human-caused deforestation, forests would cover a much greater portion of the land surface, leading to greater carbon sequestration and storage, and greater habitat for wildlife. Additionally, without human activities that alter the landscape, such as damming rivers and construction of urban areas, natural landscapes would be more intact, with more consistent patterns of river flow, water availability, and land cover.

Impact on Climate:

The absence of humans would result in significant changes to the climate of the world. Human activities, such as the burning of fossil fuels and deforestation, have greatly impacted the climate, leading to changes in temperature patterns, precipitation patterns, and atmospheric composition. In the absence of these activities, the climate would likely be much different, with more stable temperature and precipitation patterns and less atmospheric pollution.

For example, without human-caused greenhouse gas emissions, the Earth's atmosphere would contain less carbon dioxide and other heat-trapping gases, leading to a more stable climate. Additionally, without human-caused deforestation, the Earth's surface would have a greater capacity to absorb and store carbon, leading to a more balanced carbon cycle and a more stable climate.

Impact on Evolution:

The absence of humans would result in significant changes to the evolutionary trajectory of species around the world. Human activities, such as the introduction of non-native species and the exploitation of species for commercial purposes, have greatly impacted the evolution of species, leading to changes in genetic diversity, distribution patterns, and population sizes. In the absence of these activities, species would likely evolve in different ways, with different patterns of genetic diversity and population structure.

For example, without human activities that introduce non-native species, ecosystems would not be threatened by the competition and predation of introduced species, leading to more stable and diverse populations of native species. Additionally, without human activities that exploit species for commercial purposes, such as fishing and hunting, species populations would be more abundant, leading to greater genetic diversity and a more robust evolutionary trajectory.

In conclusion, the absence of humans would result in a vastly different world, with changes to biodiversity, natural processes, geography, climate, and evolution. These changes would result in greater species and ecosystem diversity, more stable natural processes, more intact natural landscapes, a more balanced climate, and a more robust evolutionary trajectory for species. It is clear that humans have a profound impact on the planet, and that our actions must be guided by a desire to preserve the delicate balance of the natural world. The study of what the world would be like without human influence provides insight into the impact of human activities and the importance of preserving and protecting the planet for future generations. By understanding the changes that would occur in the absence of humans, we can better understand the impact of our actions and work to create a more sustainable future for the planet and all its inhabitants.

CHAPTER SIX

WHAT WOULD HAPPEN IF THE EARTH'S MAGNETIC FIELD SUDDENLY FLIPPED?

Introduction:

The Earth's magnetic field is a complex and constantly changing electromagnetic force that envelops our planet. It is generated by the motion of molten iron in the Earth's core, and its shape and strength play a crucial role in protecting the planet from harmful solar and cosmic radiation, as well as guiding compasses and affecting the behavior of communication and navigation systems. The Earth's magnetic field has flipped many times in the past, with the most recent reversal occurring about 780,000 years ago. Scientists have long wondered what would happen if the magnetic field suddenly flipped again.

Body:

Impact on Earth's Atmosphere:

The Earth's magnetic field acts as a barrier to protect the planet from the harmful effects of solar and cosmic radiation. This radiation can cause changes in the composition and behavior of the Earth's atmosphere, leading to increased auroral activity, changes in atmospheric chemistry, and potentially even disruptions to weather patterns. If the magnetic field suddenly flipped, the protective barrier it provides would be weakened, exposing the planet to increased levels of harmful radiation.

This increased radiation could have significant impacts on the Earth's atmosphere, including changes in atmospheric chemistry, changes in ozone levels, and disruptions to weather patterns. For example, increased auroral activity could lead to increased atmospheric ionization, which can disrupt communication and navigation systems, particularly those that rely on low-frequency radio waves.

Impact on Life:

The Earth's magnetic field also provides a crucial shield for life on the planet. Increased levels of solar and cosmic radiation could have significant impacts on living organisms, including changes in DNA and genetic mutations, disruptions to biological processes, and reductions in population sizes. For example, increased radiation levels could lead to reductions in phytoplankton populations, which form the base of the marine food chain. This could have cascading impacts on the entire marine food web, with potentially significant impacts on global food security and ecosystems.

The increase in atmospheric ionization caused by the sudden flipping of the Earth's magnetic field could disrupt the behavior of birds and other animals that rely on the magnetic field to navigate, leading to disruptions in migration patterns and reductions in population sizes. Additionally, increased radiation levels could lead to increased rates of cancer and other health problems in humans and other animals.

Impact on Technology:

The Earth's magnetic field plays a crucial role in guiding compasses and affecting the behavior of communication and navigation systems. If the magnetic field suddenly flipped, it could cause widespread disruptions to these systems, with potentially serious consequences for global transportation, communication, and military systems. For example, GPS systems, which rely on the Earth's magnetic field for accurate positioning, could be severely impacted, leading to disruptions in transportation and other critical infrastructures.

Additionally, the increased levels of atmospheric ionization caused by the sudden flipping of the Earth's magnetic field could disrupt low-frequency radio waves, leading to widespread disruptions in communication systems. This could have serious implications for military and emergency response systems, which rely on these communications systems for effective operation.

Impact on the Earth's Surface:

The Earth's magnetic field also plays a crucial role in protecting the planet from the charged particles in the solar wind. If the magnetic field suddenly flipped, the Earth's surface could be exposed to increased levels of these charged particles, leading to increased rates of erosion and the formation of new geologic features. For example, increased erosion could lead to the formation of new river valleys and the widening of existing ones, as well as changes in the distribution of minerals and other geologic resources.

The Earth's magnetic field also affects the behavior of the planet's magnetic poles, with potential impacts on sea level and the stability of the planet's crust

The sudden flipping of the Earth's magnetic field could also have significant impacts on the planet's geomagnetic storms. Geomagnetic storms are caused by fluctuations in the Earth's magnetic field and can lead to disruptions in the electrical grid, power outages, and the failure of critical infrastructure systems. For example, geomagnetic storms have been known to cause widespread power outages, with costs in the billions of dollars in damages and lost productivity.

Additionally, the Earth's magnetic field plays a crucial role in maintaining the stability of the planet's magnetic poles. If the magnetic field suddenly flipped, it could cause significant changes in the behavior of the magnetic poles, leading to changes in sea level, the stability of the planet's crust, and the behavior of ocean currents. This could have significant impacts on global climate, including changes in temperature and precipitation patterns, and potentially even contribute to the onset of new ice ages.

Another potential impact of the sudden flipping of the Earth's magnetic field is on the planet's radiation belts. The Earth's magnetic field acts as a barrier, trapping and deflecting charged particles that would otherwise reach the surface of the planet and harm life. A sudden flip of the magnetic field could cause significant changes to the behavior of the radiation belts, potentially increasing the amount of harmful radiation reaching the surface of the planet.

Furthermore, a sudden flip of the magnetic field could also have major impacts on navigation and communication systems. The Earth's magnetic field is used by migratory animals, such as birds and sea turtles, to navigate their way through the world. It is also used by many human technologies, such as GPS and radio communication systems, which rely on a stable magnetic field to function correctly. A sudden flip of the magnetic field could disrupt these systems and lead to widespread communication and navigation failures.

Finally, the impacts of a sudden flipping of the Earth's magnetic field on human health and wellbeing should not be overlooked. Changes to the magnetic field could affect the behavior of electric currents in the body, leading to changes in the functioning of the nervous system and the cardiovascular system. This could result in increased rates of diseases such as migraines, seizures, and heart problems. Earth's magnetic field could have far-reaching and profound impacts on the planet and its inhabitants. From changes to the planet's radiation belts and the behavior of living organisms, to impacts on communication and navigation systems and human health, it is clear that a better understanding of the Earth's magnetic field and its behavior is crucial for predicting and mitigating the impacts of a sudden reversal.

The sudden flipping of the Earth's magnetic field could also have significant impacts on the planet's weather patterns. The magnetic field helps to protect the planet from solar winds, which are charged particles that are constantly blowing from the Sun. If the magnetic field were to suddenly flip, the planet would be more exposed to solar winds, which could alter atmospheric pressure and wind patterns, leading to changes in weather patterns.

Additionally, the Earth's magnetic field helps to maintain the balance between the ozone layer and the atmosphere. The ozone layer protects life on Earth from harmful UV radiation, while the atmosphere helps to regulate the planet's temperature. A sudden flip of the magnetic field could disrupt this balance, leading to changes in the behavior of the ozone layer and the atmosphere, which could contribute to global warming and other climate change effects.

It is important to note that the Earth's magnetic field has flipped many times throughout its history, and this process typically takes thousands of years to occur. However, there is evidence that the magnetic field is weakening, which could lead to a more rapid flipping of the field in the future. This is a concern, as a more rapid flipping of the magnetic field could result in more severe and widespread impacts on the planet and its inhabitants.

Finally, the impacts of a sudden flipping of the Earth's magnetic field on technology should also be considered. Many human technologies, such as power grids and communication systems, are vulnerable to the impacts of geomagnetic storms. A sudden flipping of the magnetic field could trigger intense geomagnetic storms, leading to widespread technological failures and disruptions in critical infrastructure.

It is important to note that the effects of a sudden flipping of the Earth's magnetic field would not be limited to just one region or country. Rather, the impacts would be global in scale and could have far-reaching consequences for all life on Earth. For example, the changes in weather patterns that result from the magnetic field flip could impact agriculture and food security, leading to widespread famine and malnutrition.

In addition, a sudden flipping of the magnetic field could also trigger intense geomagnetic storms, which could lead to widespread power outages and disruptions in critical infrastructure. This could impact essential services such as healthcare, communication, and transportation, leading to further widespread chaos and economic instability.

The impacts of a sudden magnetic field flip could also be compounded by other factors, such as climate change and environmental degradation. For example, rising sea levels resulting from climate change could exacerbate the impacts of coastal flooding caused by the magnetic field flip, leading to more widespread destruction and displacement of populations.

It is also important to consider the potential impacts of a sudden magnetic field flip on space exploration and satellite technology. The magnetic field helps to protect the Earth from solar and cosmic radiation, which can cause damage to spacecraft and satellites. A sudden flipping of the magnetic field could increase the exposure of spacecraft and satellites to harmful radiation, leading to increased rates of failure and loss of these critical technologies.

It is also important to consider the impact that a sudden flipping of the magnetic field would have on wildlife and ecosystems. The magnetic field helps to regulate the migration patterns of many species, including birds and sea turtles, which navigate using the Earth's magnetic field as a guide. A sudden flipping of the magnetic field could disrupt the migration patterns of these species, leading to population declines and loss of biodiversity.

In addition, the changes in atmospheric pressure and wind patterns that result from a magnetic field flip could also impact the behavior of ocean currents, leading to changes in ocean temperatures and salinity. This could have significant impacts on marine ecosystems and the species that depend on them, leading to declines in population sizes and loss of biodiversity.

Furthermore, a sudden flipping of the magnetic field could also increase the exposure of life on Earth to harmful cosmic radiation. This could result in increased rates of genetic mutations, leading to the evolution of new species, as well as increased rates of cancer and other health effects for humans and other species.

Another factor to consider is the impact of a sudden magnetic field flip on human societies and cultures. Throughout history, humans have used the Earth's magnetic field as a reference for navigation and exploration, and a sudden flipping of the magnetic field could lead to widespread confusion and disorientation. Additionally, the widespread power outages and disruptions to essential services that result from a magnetic field flip could trigger widespread panic, leading to social unrest and instability.

One of the major concerns regarding the sudden flipping of the Earth's magnetic field is the potential impact on the electrical power grid. The magnetic field helps to protect the Earth from the effects of solar storms, which can cause surges of electrical energy to flow through power lines and cause widespread power outages. A sudden flipping of the magnetic field could result in an increase in the frequency and intensity of these solar storms, leading to widespread and prolonged power outages, as well as damage to electrical transformers and other critical components of the electrical power grid.

Additionally, a sudden magnetic field flip could also impact the performance of navigation systems, such as GPS and other satellite-based navigation systems. The magnetic field helps to shield the Earth from solar and cosmic radiation, which can interfere with the performance of these navigation systems. A sudden flipping of the magnetic field could increase the exposure of these navigation systems to harmful radiation, leading to decreased accuracy and increased risk of failure.

Another important factor to consider is the impact of a sudden magnetic field flip on the communication systems that support modern society. The magnetic field helps to protect the Earth from harmful ionizing radiation, which can interfere with the performance of communication systems, such as radio and television signals, and even cause widespread blackouts. A sudden flipping of the magnetic field could increase the exposure of these communication systems to harmful ionizing radiation, leading to widespread disruptions in communication and loss of access to critical information.

A sudden magnetic field flip could also have implications for the exploration of space and the study of the solar system. The magnetic field helps to protect the Earth from harmful solar and cosmic radiation, which can impact the performance of spacecraft and satellites. A sudden flipping of the magnetic field could increase the exposure of these spacecraft and satellites to harmful radiation, leading to increased rates of failure and decreased scientific understanding of the solar system and the universe.

The sudden flipping of the Earth's magnetic field could also have implications for the planet's climate and ecosystems. The magnetic field helps to protect the Earth from harmful solar and cosmic radiation, which can impact the planet's atmosphere and trigger significant changes in climate patterns. A sudden flipping of the magnetic field could increase the exposure of the planet to harmful radiation, leading to increased rates of atmospheric and climatic changes.

One potential consequence of these changes is the disruption of ocean currents and the food chain. The ocean currents are driven by differences in temperature and salinity, which are in turn influenced by changes in the Earth's climate patterns. A sudden flipping of the magnetic field could trigger significant changes in the ocean currents, leading to disruptions in the food chain and changes in the distribution and abundance of marine life

Another impact of a sudden magnetic field flip could be the increase in the number of auroras and other geomagnetic phenomena. Auroras are caused by charged particles from the sun entering the Earth's magnetic field and colliding with atmospheric particles. A sudden flipping of the magnetic field could result in an increase in the number and intensity of auroras, potentially leading to increased radiation exposure for humans and wildlife in high-latitude regions.

It is also possible that a sudden magnetic field flip could impact the stability of the Earth's crust and trigger earthquakes and volcanic activity. The magnetic field is thought to play a role in maintaining the stability of the Earth's crust, and a sudden change in the magnetic field could cause instability and increase the risk of earthquakes and volcanic activity.

Finally, a sudden magnetic field flip could have significant impacts on human society and civilization. The widespread disruptions in the electrical power grid, navigation systems, and communication systems could lead to economic and social instability, as well as loss of life and property. Additionally, the impacts on the planet's climate and ecosystems could lead to changes in the distribution and abundance of resources, and potentially even the extinction of certain species.

Additionally, a sudden magnetic field flip could also have implications for the accuracy of navigation systems. Modern navigation systems rely on the Earth's magnetic field to provide an accurate sense of direction, and a sudden flip could throw off these systems and cause significant disruptions to transportation and commerce. This could have major impacts on the global economy, as well as on individual communities and businesses that rely on accurate navigation for their operations.

A sudden magnetic field flip could also lead to disruptions in the Earth's ozone layer, which protects the planet from harmful ultraviolet radiation. The ozone layer is maintained by a delicate balance of atmospheric processes, and a sudden change in the magnetic field could disrupt this balance and lead to increased rates of ozone depletion. This in turn could lead to increased exposure to harmful ultraviolet radiation, which could have negative impacts on human health and wildlife populations.

In addition to these impacts, a sudden magnetic field flip could also have implications for the stability of the Earth's atmosphere. The magnetic field helps to shield the Earth from charged particles that are constantly bombarding the planet from space. A sudden flip could disrupt this shielding effect, leading to increased rates of atmospheric ionization and potentially even the loss of the Earth's atmosphere over time.

To sum up, the potential impacts of a sudden magnetic field flip are complex and far-reaching, and could have major consequences for the planet's climate and ecosystems, human society and civilization, and the stability of the Earth's atmosphere. Further research and understanding of the Earth's magnetic field are necessary in order to better predict and prepare for the potential impacts of a sudden magnetic field flip.

It is also important to note that a sudden magnetic field flip could have long-term effects on the Earth's climate. The magnetic field helps to protect the planet from cosmic rays and solar wind, which can contribute to the formation of clouds and precipitation. A sudden change in the magnetic field could alter these processes and potentially lead to changes in the Earth's climate, including changes in atmospheric circulation, temperature patterns, and precipitation levels. These climate changes could have far-reaching impacts on ecosystems, agriculture, and human societies, particularly in regions that are already vulnerable to the impacts of climate change.

Another potential impact of a sudden magnetic field flip is increased exposure to radiation. Cosmic rays and solar wind can pose a health risk to astronauts and other people living in high-altitude or high-latitude regions, and a sudden change in the magnetic field could lead to increased exposure to these harmful particles. Additionally, a sudden magnetic field flip could increase the risk of power grid failures, as well as disrupt other electrical systems, such as those used in hospitals and other critical infrastructure. This could have major impacts on human health and safety, and could also lead to widespread economic and social disruptions.

Finally, a sudden magnetic field flip could also have implications for the migration patterns of wildlife and birds. Many species, such as birds and sea turtles, rely on the Earth's magnetic field for navigation and homing, and a sudden change in the magnetic field could disorient these animals and cause significant disruptions to their migration patterns. This could have negative impacts on the populations of these species, as well as on the ecosystems and communities that depend on them.

In conclusion, a sudden reversal of the Earth's magnetic field could have profound and far-reaching impacts on the planet and its inhabitants. A weakened magnetic field could lead to increased exposure to cosmic rays and solar wind, which could pose a threat to human health and critical infrastructure. It could also impact navigation systems, disrupt migration patterns for wildlife, and potentially alter the Earth's climate. While the exact effects of a sudden magnetic field flip are difficult to predict, it is clear that this event would have significant consequences for the Earth and its ecosystems. Further research and understanding of the Earth's magnetic field are necessary in order to better predict and prepare for the potential impacts of such an event.

CHAPTER SEVEN

Can we theoretically create a black hole on Earth and if so, what would happen?

Black holes are mysterious and enigmatic objects that have captured the imagination of scientists and the public alike. They are formed when massive stars collapse in on themselves, creating regions of space where the gravitational pull is so strong that not even light can escape. Despite their reputation as cosmic monsters, black holes also play a crucial role in our understanding of the universe, providing us with valuable information about the evolution of galaxies and the behavior of matter and energy under extreme conditions.

Recently, there has been growing interest in the possibility of creating a black hole on Earth. This idea is rooted in the concept of artificial black holes, which are theoretical objects that could be created by compressing matter to incredibly high densities. But can we really create a black hole on Earth, and if so, what would happen?

Theoretical Possibilities of Creating a Black Hole on Earth:

The idea of creating a black hole on Earth is based on the fact that black holes are formed by the collapse of massive objects, such as stars. If we could somehow create an object with sufficient mass and compress it to a small enough size, we might be able to create an artificial black hole. This is easier said than done, however, as the process of creating a black hole would require enormous amounts of energy and a deep understanding of the behavior of matter and energy under extreme conditions.

One possibility for creating a black hole on Earth is through the use of particle accelerators. Particle accelerators work by accelerating particles to nearly the speed of light and then colliding them with each other. When these particles collide, they release large amounts of energy, which could potentially be used to create a black hole. However, the energy required to create a black hole in this way would be enormous, and it is currently beyond our technological capabilities to generate such a large amount of energy.

Another possibility for creating a black hole on Earth is through the use of gravitational waves. Gravitational waves are ripples in the fabric of space-time that are created by the acceleration of massive objects. If we could generate a large enough gravitational wave, we might be able to create an artificial black hole. This would require a deep understanding of the behavior of gravitational waves and a significant technological advance in our ability to generate and control these waves.

What Would Happen if a Black Hole was Created on Earth:

If we were able to create a black hole on Earth, there would be significant consequences for our planet and its inhabitants. First and foremost, the black hole would pose a threat to human life, as its gravitational pull would be so strong that anything within its reach would be pulled in and destroyed. This would include cities, buildings, and entire populations.

Additionally, a black hole on Earth would alter our planet's climate and weather patterns. The black hole's gravitational pull would affect the Earth's atmosphere and ocean currents, leading to changes in precipitation patterns, temperature patterns, and other meteorological phenomena.

Furthermore, a black hole on Earth would also impact our ability to communicate and navigate. The black hole's strong gravitational pull would disrupt radio waves, GPS signals, and other forms of communication, making it difficult or impossible to communicate with other parts of the world.

Theoretical Possibility of Creating a Black Hole on Earth

One of the key requirements for creating a black hole is to have a large enough amount of mass or energy compressed into a small enough space. A black hole forms when a massive object collapses in on itself, creating an area of space-time from which not even light can escape. In the case of creating a black hole on Earth, there are some challenges that would need to be overcome.

First, it would require an enormous amount of mass to be compressed into a tiny volume. For example, if we were to compress all of the mass of the Earth into a space the size of a sugar cube, a black hole would form. This is not practical with our current technology and knowledge.

Second, we would need to find a way to overcome the immense gravitational forces that would be present during the collapse. These forces would be so great that they would cause the material to shatter into smaller pieces, making it much more difficult to form a stable black hole.

Finally, even if it were possible to create a black hole on Earth, there is no guarantee that it would remain stable. Black holes are extremely dynamic objects that can change rapidly in size and shape, and any fluctuations could cause the black hole to destabilize and possibly even disintegrate.

Consequences of a Black Hole on Earth

If it were possible to create a black hole on Earth, the consequences would be catastrophic. The immense gravitational pull of a black hole would cause everything within its event horizon, the point of no return, to be sucked in and potentially destroyed. This includes all of the Earth's oceans, land masses, and atmosphere.

In addition to the destruction of the planet, the creation of a black hole on Earth would also have a profound effect on the surrounding solar system. The black hole's gravity would disrupt the orbits of nearby planets, potentially sending them careening into the sun or out into the depths of space. This could have far-reaching consequences for the entire solar system and could even impact the stability of the Milky Way galaxy as a whole.

It is also important to note that black holes emit high-energy particles known as Hawking radiation, which could be potentially harmful to life on Earth. If a black hole were to be created on the planet, it is likely that the intense radiation it would emit would sterilize the planet and make it uninhabitable for millions of years, if not forever.

Factors Limiting the Creation of a Black Hole on Earth

One of the main limitations to creating a black hole on Earth is the sheer amount of energy and mass that would be required. In order to create a black hole, a sufficient amount of mass must be compressed into a small enough space that the gravitational forces it generates are strong enough to trap light. For this to happen on Earth, a large portion of the planet would need to be compressed into an area much smaller than the size of a sugar cube.

In addition to the mass requirements, there are also technological limitations that would need to be overcome. To compress such a large amount of matter, a tremendous amount of energy would be required. This energy would need to be generated in a way that is controllable and predictable, so that the material could be compressed into a stable black hole. This is a challenging task, given that the energy involved would be many orders of magnitude greater than what we are currently capable of generating and controlling.

Finally, even if we were able to overcome these technological limitations, the formation of a black hole on Earth would likely be unstable. Black holes are known for their extreme instability, and any fluctuations in their size or shape could cause them to destabilize and potentially even disintegrate. This would result in the release of an enormous amount of energy, which could have catastrophic consequences for the planet and its inhabitants.

The dangers of Black Holes

While the creation of a black hole on Earth is highly unlikely, it is still important to understand the dangers that black holes pose. For one, the intense gravitational pull of a black hole could cause it to suck in everything within its event horizon, including stars, planets, and even entire galaxies.

In addition to this, black holes also emit high-energy particles known as Hawking radiation. These particles are potentially harmful to life and could sterilize a planet, making it uninhabitable for millions of years.

Furthermore, black holes are known to have a profound impact on their surrounding environment. The intense gravitational pull of a black hole can disrupt the orbits of nearby objects, potentially sending them careening into the sun or out into the depths of space. This can have far-reaching consequences for the stability of entire galaxies and could impact the development of life in the universe.

In conclusion, while the creation of a black hole on Earth is highly unlikely, it is still important to understand the dangers that black holes pose and the potential impact they can have on their surroundings. Further research into black holes and their effects on the universe is necessary in order to fully understand and mitigate these dangers.

Alternative Theories to Black Hole Formation

While the creation of a black hole on Earth through compression is highly unlikely, there are alternative theories that suggest the formation of black holes in other ways. For example, some theories suggest that black holes could be formed through the collision of two neutron stars. Neutron stars are extremely dense objects that are formed from the remnants of supernovae. When two neutron stars collide, the intense gravitational forces generated could cause the stars to collapse into a single, highly compressed object known as a black hole.

Another alternative theory suggests that black holes could be formed from the collapse of massive clouds of gas and dust. This process, known as gravitational collapse, occurs when the gravitational forces within a cloud of gas and dust become so strong that they cause the cloud to collapse in on itself. If the cloud is large enough, the collapse could continue until a black hole is formed.

Finally, some theories suggest that black holes could be formed through the accretion of matter onto a compact object, such as a neutron star or a white dwarf. As matter is drawn onto the compact object, it becomes increasingly dense and compressed, eventually forming a black hole.

In all of these alternative theories, the formation of a black hole would likely still require a significant amount of energy and mass. However, the processes involved may be different than those involved in the creation of a black hole through compression.

Impact of Black Holes on Our Understanding of the Universe

Despite the difficulties involved in creating a black hole on Earth, the study of black holes has had a profound impact on our understanding of the universe. Black holes provide us with a unique window into the most extreme environments in the universe, allowing us to study the behavior of matter and energy under conditions that cannot be replicated in any other way.

Through the study of black holes, we have learned about the properties of space and time, the nature of matter and energy, and the evolution of galaxies and the universe as a whole. Black holes have also helped us to better understand the process of gravitational collapse and the role that gravity plays in shaping the universe.

In addition to these fundamental discoveries, black holes have also been used to test some of the most fundamental theories of physics, such as Einstein's theory of general relativity and quantum mechanics. By observing the behavior of matter and energy near black holes, scientists have been able to put these theories to the test and gain new insights into the nature of the universe

If the creation of a black hole on Earth were possible, it would have disastrous consequences. The intense gravitational pull of a black hole would cause everything within its event horizon to be pulled in, including the entire planet. This would result in the destruction of the Earth and potentially the entire solar system.

Furthermore, the creation of a black hole on Earth would also have a significant impact on the fabric of space-time. According to Einstein's theory of general relativity, massive objects like black holes curve space-time. If a black hole were created on Earth, the strong curvature of space-time around it could potentially cause ripples in the fabric of space-time, known as gravitational waves. These waves could then propagate throughout the universe, potentially causing devastating effects on other celestial objects.

In addition to the physical effects, a black hole on Earth would also have serious implications for life on our planet. The intense gravitational pull of the black hole would cause massive tidal waves and earthquakes, potentially wiping out all life on Earth. The intense radiation produced by the black hole would also have devastating effects on the atmosphere, potentially causing widespread ozone depletion and altering the climate.

However, it is important to note that the creation of a black hole on Earth is purely theoretical and highly unlikely to occur in reality. According to current scientific understanding, the conditions required to create a black hole are found only in the extreme environments of space, such as the centers of galaxies or the aftermath of a supernova.

Even if these conditions were somehow recreated on Earth, the amount of energy required to create a black hole would be immense and far beyond our current technological capabilities. For example, to create a black hole with a mass equivalent to that of the Earth, an amount of energy equivalent to the mass of the Earth would need to be concentrated into a single point. This is a physical impossibility, as such a concentration of energy would result in a singularity, a point in space-time where the laws of physics as we know them break down.

Despite the theoretical difficulties, the idea of creating a black hole on Earth continues to captivate the imagination of scientists and the public alike. Theoretical physicists have even proposed the existence of "micro black holes", which would be much smaller and less massive than traditional black holes. However, even the creation of a micro black hole on Earth is highly unlikely, and the potential consequences of such an event are not well understood.

One of the main concerns regarding the creation of a black hole on Earth is the potential for it to consume nearby matter, including entire planets or stars. The intense gravitational pull of a black hole could cause significant damage to the surrounding environment, potentially even leading to the destruction of our solar system.

Additionally, black holes are believed to emit high levels of radiation, which could have a significant impact on life on Earth. The intense radiation emitted by a black hole could potentially cause widespread damage to the ozone layer, leading to increased levels of ultraviolet radiation reaching the surface of the Earth. This could have devastating effects on living organisms, potentially leading to widespread extinctions.

It is also worth considering the ethical and philosophical implications of the creation of a black hole on Earth. The creation of a black hole would represent a profound shift in our understanding of the universe, and raise questions about the limits of human knowledge and technology. Some have even argued that such an event could have profound spiritual or religious implications, leading to a rethinking of our place in the cosmos.

In conclusion, the theoretical creation of a black hole on Earth is a fascinating but highly unlikely scenario. While the potential consequences of such an event are not well understood, it is clear that the creation of a black hole would represent a significant shift in our understanding of the universe and have profound implications for life on Earth. Despite the theoretical difficulties and unknown consequences, the idea of creating a black hole on Earth continues to captivate the imagination of scientists and the public alike.

CHAPTER EIGHT

If Aliens Existed, What Scientific Evidence Could We Use to Detect Their Presence?

The existence of extraterrestrial life has been a topic of speculation and debate for centuries, and the search for evidence of their existence has been ongoing for many years. While there is currently no concrete evidence that aliens exist, the possibility that they do has driven numerous scientific endeavors and theories. If aliens do exist, the question of how to detect their presence becomes a critical one. In this chapter, we will explore the potential scientific evidence that could be used to detect the presence of extraterrestrial life.

Direct Evidence:

One of the most direct ways to detect the presence of aliens is through the detection of their signals. This can be accomplished through the use of radio telescopes, which are capable of detecting radio signals that are transmitted from distant objects. Radio telescopes have been used for many years to search for extraterrestrial life and have so far found no evidence of their existence. However, the search continues, and new technologies are being developed to make the search for extraterrestrial life more effective.

Indirect Evidence:

Another way to detect the presence of aliens is through the detection of their physical or biological signatures. This could involve looking for signs of alien technology, such as artifacts or structures, or looking for signs of life, such as organic molecules or atmospheric biosignatures. For example, the presence of an atmosphere containing oxygen would be an indirect sign of life, as oxygen is typically produced by living organisms. The detection of organic molecules in the atmospheres of exoplanets could also be an indirect sign of life.

Astrobiological Evidence:

Another way to detect the presence of extraterrestrial life is through the study of astrobiology. This field of study involves the examination of the conditions necessary for life to exist, such as the presence of water, suitable temperatures, and appropriate atmospheric conditions. By studying these conditions on other planets and moons, scientists can determine the likelihood of life existing on those objects and search for evidence of its presence.

Various scientific methods can be used to search for evidence of extraterrestrial life. These include:

Spectroscopy: The study of the interaction of light with matter can provide clues about the composition of planets and moons in our solar system and beyond. Scientists can analyze the light from stars and look for specific spectral lines that indicate the presence of certain chemicals such as water, oxygen, and methane. If the light from a distant planet shows evidence of these chemicals, it is possible that life exists there.

Remote Sensing: Advanced telescopes and satellites can be used to observe the surface features and atmospheres of exoplanets. By analyzing the light that is reflected or absorbed by these planets, scientists can determine if they have the right conditions to support life, such as a stable climate and the presence of water.

SETI (Search for Extraterrestrial Intelligence): This is the search for signals from extraterrestrial civilizations that may be transmitted through radio or laser signals. Scientists have been listening for signals from space for decades and have not yet detected any definitive evidence of extraterrestrial life.

Biosignatures: Scientists can look for signs of life on exoplanets by analyzing the chemical composition of their atmospheres. For example, if an atmosphere contains a large amount of oxygen, this could be a sign that life exists, as oxygen is produced by photosynthetic organisms. Other gases, such as methane, can also be indicative of life, as it is produced by microbes on Earth.

Another method for detecting extraterrestrial life is through the study of exoplanet habitability. The habitability of exoplanets can be assessed by examining factors such as the distance from their star, the presence of liquid water, and the atmospheric conditions. If a planet has conditions similar to those of Earth, it is considered to be a potentially habitable planet, and scientists can study it further to determine if life may exist there.

In addition to searching for signs of extraterrestrial life on exoplanets, scientists are also looking for evidence of extraterrestrial life in our own solar system. For example, they are studying the conditions on Mars and other moons in the solar system to determine if they may have supported life in the past or if they could support life in the future.

Another area of research is astrobiology, which is the study of the origin, evolution, and distribution of life in the universe. This field combines biology, astronomy, and geology to understand the conditions under which life can emerge and evolve. Scientists are using astrobiological studies to determine what types of environments and conditions are most conducive to the development of life, and to determine the likelihood of finding life elsewhere in the universe.

Finally, the detection of biosignatures is another potential method for detecting extraterrestrial life. Biosignatures are specific chemical or physical indicators that suggest the presence of life. For example, the presence of certain organic molecules, such as methane or carbon dioxide, could be a biosignature, as these are often associated with life. Another potential biosignature is the presence of oxygen in a planet's atmosphere, as this gas is produced by photosynthetic organisms. Scientists are also searching for variations in a planet's light or spectrum that may indicate the presence of life.

In order to detect these biosignatures, scientists use a variety of instruments and techniques, including remote sensing and spectroscopy. Remote sensing is the measurement of electromagnetic radiation emitted by an object. By analyzing the light and radiation emitted by a planet, scientists can determine its chemical composition and other important characteristics. Spectroscopy is the study of the interaction between light and matter. By analyzing the light that passes through a planet's atmosphere, scientists can determine its chemical makeup and search for signs of life.

The search for extraterrestrial life is also being pursued by searching for technological signals, such as radio waves or other forms of communication, that may have been generated by extraterrestrial civilizations. This method is known as the Search for Extraterrestrial Intelligence (SETI) and it has been ongoing for several decades. SETI programs use large radio telescopes to listen for signals from extraterrestrial civilizations and to search for evidence of their existence. The search for extraterrestrial life is a multifaceted and ongoing effort that is being pursued by scientists around the world. The detection of extraterrestrial life would have profound implications for our understanding of the universe and our place within it. Whether we find evidence of extraterrestrial life or not, the search will continue to reveal new and exciting information about the universe and our place within it.

One potential scientific method for detecting the presence of extraterrestrial life is the search for biosignatures in the atmosphere of exoplanets. Biosignatures are gases that are produced by living organisms, such as oxygen, methane, and nitrogen, which can be detected through spectroscopy. If a planet with an atmosphere contains a high concentration of certain biosignatures, it is possible that the source of these gases could be extraterrestrial life.

Another way to detect the presence of aliens is through the search for artificial signals or technological artifacts.

The SETI (Search for Extraterrestrial Intelligence) program uses radio telescopes to listen for radio signals that may be emanating from extraterrestrial civilizations. In addition, researchers are also searching for artificial structures or artifacts that may be orbiting other stars or located in our own solar system.

A third way to detect the presence of extraterrestrial life is through the study of extremophiles, or organisms that can survive in extreme environments. The discovery of such life on Earth or in our solar system could provide evidence that life may be abundant in the universe. For example, the discovery of microbial life in subglacial lakes on Earth has led scientists to search for similar life forms on other icy moons in our solar system.

Another approach to detect extraterrestrial life is through the search for astrobiological evidence on other planets and moons. This includes looking for signs of liquid water, as water is believed to be a key requirement for life as we know it. The presence of water can be detected through various methods, including the measurement of hydrogen in the atmosphere, the examination of mineral deposits, and the analysis of spectral data. For example, the Mars Reconnaissance Orbiter has been used to search for evidence of liquid water on Mars, while the Galileo spacecraft has been used to study the icy moons of Jupiter for signs of subsurface oceans.

In addition, the search for extraterrestrial life can also involve the study of planet formation and the detection of habitable exoplanets. The study of planet formation helps us understand how planetary systems and habitable zones form and evolve, while the detection of habitable exoplanets involves looking for planets in the habitable zones of their stars, where conditions are potentially suitable for life. This includes the use of transit photometry, radial velocity, and direct imaging methods to detect exoplanets and study their atmospheres.

The search for extraterrestrial life can also involve the study of the distribution of elements in the universe and the formation of organic compounds. The distribution of elements is important because the elements that are necessary for life are distributed throughout the universe. The formation of organic compounds is also critical, as these compounds are the building blocks of life. The study of organic compounds can be done through spectroscopic analysis, which involves the study of the light that is emitted or absorbed by a molecule.

While searching for extraterrestrial life, scientists and researchers have proposed a number of methods for detecting the presence of aliens. These methods are based on the assumption that any advanced extraterrestrial civilization would likely produce certain signs that we could detect with our current technology.

One such method is the search for electromagnetic signals. Radio telescopes on Earth are used to search for radio signals that may be coming from extraterrestrial civilizations. The most well-known example of this is the SETI (Search for Extraterrestrial Intelligence) project, which has been scanning the skies for signals since the 1960s. However, to date, no signals have been conclusively confirmed as coming from extraterrestrial civilizations.

Another method is the search for biomarkers. This involves looking for chemical evidence of life on other planets, such as the presence of water, oxygen, or organic molecules. The study of exoplanets, or planets outside of our solar system, has made significant progress in recent years and several potentially habitable exoplanets have been discovered. This has raised the possibility that life may exist elsewhere in the universe.

A third method is the search for anomalies in celestial objects. This involves looking for any unusual or unexpected features or behavior of celestial objects, such as stars or galaxies, that might indicate the presence of extraterrestrial civilizations. For example, some researchers have suggested that the strange behavior of Tabby's Star, a star that has been observed to periodically dim, might be the result of an alien megastructure blocking its light.

Additionally, scientists have proposed the idea of using gravitational lensing to detect extraterrestrial civilizations. This involves observing the distortions in light from distant stars that are caused by the gravitational pull of massive celestial objects, such as black holes or alien megastructures. This technique has not yet been used to search for extraterrestrial life, but it holds promise for the future.

The study of astrobiology, which is the science of life in the universe, has brought up a lot of interesting questions regarding the possibility of life beyond our planet. If aliens existed, what scientific evidence could we use to detect their presence? There are a number of possible methods that have been proposed to look for evidence of extraterrestrial life, including searching for signals that could have been transmitted by civilizations, looking for changes in the light of distant stars that might be caused by orbiting exoplanets, and analyzing the chemical composition of planets and moons in our solar system to see if they contain the building blocks of life.

One method that has gained a lot of attention in recent years is the search for extraterrestrial signals, or messages that could have been transmitted from civilizations elsewhere in the universe. This search is conducted by SETI (Search for Extraterrestrial Intelligence), an organization that uses telescopes and other scientific instruments to listen for possible signals from other civilizations. SETI has found no evidence of extraterrestrial life thus far, but the search is ongoing and many scientists believe that it is only a matter of time before we detect a signal from another civilization.

Another possible method of detecting alien life is by looking for changes in the light of distant stars, which could be caused by the presence of exoplanets orbiting the star. Scientists use telescopes and other instruments to measure the brightness and color of the light that is emitted by these stars, and they look for changes that might indicate the presence of a planet. This method is called the transit method, and it has been used to discover a large number of exoplanets in recent years. Scientists are now using this method to search for signs of life on these exoplanets, such as the presence of an atmosphere that could contain oxygen or other gases that are indicative of life.

A third possible method of detecting alien life is by analyzing the chemical composition of planets and moons in our solar system to see if they contain the building blocks of life. Scientists use telescopes and other instruments to measure the chemical composition of the surfaces of these objects, and they look for the presence of organic molecules, such as amino acids, that are essential for life. This method is called astrochemistry, and it is one of the most promising ways of searching for evidence of life elsewhere in the universe.

In recent years, researchers have developed a number of methods to detect possible evidence of extraterrestrial life, which could be applied to search for evidence of aliens. One of the main tools used to detect aliens is the search for bio-signatures, or chemical markers of life, in the atmospheres of exoplanets. This is done by using spectroscopy, which is a method that allows scientists to study the chemical composition of planets and moons by analyzing the light they reflect and emit. For example, the presence of oxygen, ozone, and methane in a planet's atmosphere could suggest that life exists there, as these molecules can only be produced by living organisms.

Another way scientists look for evidence of aliens is through the search for technological signals, such as radio waves or laser emissions, which could be produced by an extraterrestrial civilization. The SETI (Search for Extraterrestrial Intelligence) program, for example, scans the sky for radio signals that might come from extraterrestrial civilizations. Scientists also look for evidence of structures built by aliens, such as artificial satellites or megastructures, around other stars.

Finally, scientists are also looking for evidence of past or present life on other bodies within our own solar system, such as Mars, Europa, or Enceladus. This could be done through the study of rocks, minerals, and ice samples collected by lander missions and rovers, as well as through the analysis of data collected by remote sensing missions. For example, scientists have recently found evidence of liquid water and organic molecules on Mars, which are both important ingredients for life, and are now investigating whether life ever existed on the Red Planet.

In conclusion, the existence of extraterrestrial life is still a mystery, but if aliens existed, scientists could use a variety of evidence to detect their presence. This could include the search for biosignatures in exoplanets, the observation of unusual spectral features in light emitted by other stars, or the detection of communication signals from advanced civilizations. While the search for aliens is still ongoing and there is currently no concrete evidence of extraterrestrial life, scientists continue to explore the universe in search of answers. With advancements in technology, the ability to detect alien life has improved, and it is possible that one day we will discover definitive proof of extraterrestrial life. Until then, the possibility of alien life continues to inspire the imagination and drive scientific inquiry.

Printed by Libri Plureos GmbH in Hamburg, Germany